Between Two Worlds

Cowley Publications is a ministry of the brothers of the Society of Saint John the Evangelist, a monastic order in the Episcopal Church. Our mission is to provide books and resources for those seeking spiritual and theological formation. Cowley Publications is committed to developing a new generation of writers and teachers who will encourage people to think and pray in new ways about spirituality, reconciliation, and the future.

Between Two Worlds

Daily Readings for Advent

Kate Moorehead

A COWLEY PUBLICATIONS BOOK

Lanham, Chicago, New York, Toronto, and Plymouth, UK

Published by Cowley Publications
An imprint of Rowman & Littlefield Publishers, Inc.
A wholly owned subsidiary of The Rowman & Littlefield Publishing Group, Inc.
4501 Forbes Boulevard, Suite 200
Lanham, MD 20706

Estover Road
Plymouth PL6 7PY
United Kingdom

Distributed by National Book Network

Library of Congress Cataloging-in-Publication Data
Moorehead, Katherine Bingham, 1970–

    Between two worlds : daily readings for Advent

       p.   cm.

Summary:

    ISBN 1-56101-221-1 (pbk. : alk. paper)

    1. Advent 2. Devotional calendars. I. Title.

BV40.M66 2003

242'.332—dc22   2003021235

Cover design: Gary Ragaglia

Printed in the United States of America.

♾™
    The paper used in this publication meets the minimum requirements of
American National Standard for Information Sciences—Permanence of
Paper for Printed Library Materials, ANSI/NISO Z39.48-1992.

In memory of my father-in-law, the Rev. J. Donald Moorehead, a Methodist pastor for forty-seven years. In his life, he pursued justice and truth. I will always miss you, Don.

Table of Contents

Foreword

We know that the Feast of the Incarnation—Christmas—is not, strictly speaking, the heavy hitter of the Christian year. That's Easter. We know that the Puritans didn't celebrate Christmas, for fear that somebody somewhere might have some fun, and that it was not really until the nineteenth century that popular observance of Christmas began to reach its current immensity.

But knowing these sober facts doesn't help us: we swim in popular culture, and the run-up to Christmas is, for many good people, a cacophony of competing demands. Make it perfect, wrap it up and mail it, stir it up, cut it out and bake it, learn it and sing it, write it and preach it, stuff it and roast it. If all else fails, kiss it under the mistletoe.

Into all this noise comes Kate Moorehead. Priest and mom. Mom and priest. These two take turns wearing the initial capital letter, jockeying for position several times an hour. But you don't have to be a priest or a mom to feel the pressure of this holiday season. And anyone can reach for the remedy. What we really need to keep in mind is who we are, and *whose* we are. That done, the merely urgent will separate on its own from the really important, and we will know what we can put aside.

This book will help. We need to find a moment or two in which we can put it all aside with Kate, as she must do if she is to survive Advent without going nuts. She wants more from these four weeks than just to survive them, and so do we. Let them be sprinkled with these meditations and some quiet time—even just a little—and we will be ready to welcome Christ once more.

Barbara Cawthorne Crafton
The Geranium Farm

Introduction

It is the twenty-first century, and our lives have never been faster. The rise of information technology, initially created to make our lives easier, has increased both the speed of communication and the expectation of productivity. Never before have human beings been able to hurtle themselves through space at such speed. Never before have we been able to send the written word thousands of miles in a matter of seconds. Never have we accomplished more, and yet never has peace of mind been further from the human experience. We are becoming so accustomed to the increased pace of our lives that our minds race even when we find a quiet moment.

As a full-time parish priest and the mother of two toddlers, I am as busy as they come. There are many days when I am forced to feed my children in the car on the way to a meeting or appointment. In fact, we spend so much time in the car that it's beginning to feel like a second home. And I know that our experience is not the exception, but the norm. It is simply impossible to live in our culture and not experience the rush of America. Like a plague, it sweeps across our land touching almost every home. And we all have bought into the myth. We brag to one another about our busy lives, equating busyness with productivity, with liveliness, even with success.

Busyness, however, is the greatest sin of the twenty-first century, making us feel productive when, all the while, we are running from ourselves and, more importantly, from God.

In a nation of fast food where speed is a valued commodity, the season of Advent comes like the unwanted stepchild. The word *advent* means "coming." Advent is the season preceding Christmas. The four Sundays of Advent are always the four Sundays before Christmas Day. Advent ushers in the beginning of the Christian year. Advent is all about waiting for Christ to come. Advent is a season of waiting.

But who wants to wait in today's age? Whenever we are forced to wait, it means that the service must be poor, that there must be some sort of problem. Waiting is a sign of failure. The faster something is produced, the better for our convenience. No one wants to wait in a traffic jam. No one wants to wait when someone is late. No one wants to wait.

Yet even today, we cannot deny that most things of true value take time to come. I waited nine months for each of my children to be born. Nine months of preparation, careful eating, and something growing inside of me. There are even a few fine restaurants where one still can order dinner and expect to wait. And that waiting, perhaps over some good wine, is part of an older, wiser expectation of quality. Somewhere in the back of the human psyche, we still remember that the best food takes time to prepare.

On an even grander scale, the works of creation have all

taken time. They have taken time beyond our knowing, beyond our understanding. The highest mountains have taken eons to emerge. The human race itself may have developed over millions of years. Many theologians now understand that one day in the mind of God may be the equivalent of one billion human years. Indeed, the Divine Creator's work often takes time: the slow, progressive healing of a wound, the growth of a seed, the development of the human mind. If we are to see the hand of God in the world about us, it is often necessary to slow down, watch, and wait.

I would press on to say that everything of value in our human existence takes time. From the birth of a child to the fostering of relationships, from the acquisition of knowledge to the development of skills, most truly valued things take time to develop. That is why the highest educational degrees take the most time to earn. It is the investment of time itself, just as much as the accumulated knowledge, that makes the degree valued and respected.

And why should we not be expected to wait for the coming of Christ? Is not the Incarnation the most cherished, most anticipated of events for all Christians? Of course we are asked to wait. Our waiting is a sign of our love for Christ, our value of his presence. God asks us to wait because we need to learn the importance of not being instantly gratified. God asks us to wait because we must realize that God exists in a time far beyond the scope of our understanding. God asks us to wait because the Beloved is worth it. The discipline of waiting teaches us the value of the One for whom we must wait.

C. S. Lewis, a great Anglican theologian, wrote many books and treatises on the nature of God. However, one of his most profound theological insights came not when he was theorizing, but when he was pouring out his grief over the death of his wife, Joye. Lewis lived as a bachelor for many years. He did not meet Joye until later in his life, and by that time, he had begun to believe that he never would marry, that there simply was not a woman made who could satisfy his hunger, who could fill his heart. Joye was already diagnosed with cancer when they met. But they fell in love nonetheless. Her cancer went into a short remission, giving the couple a few brief years together. These were the most beautiful years of Lewis's life. Their love for each other was potent.

Upon the death of his wife, Lewis had to come to grips with the fact that God had given him love and then taken it away. Why did he have to lose her? Why must he now wait for the day when he might see her again? Was there any Divine purpose at all? In a small book called *A Grief Observed,* Lewis wrote:

> If, as I can't help suspecting, the dead also feel the pains of separation (and this may be one of their purgatorial sufferings), then for both lovers, and for all pairs of lovers without exception, bereavement is a universal and integral part of our experience of love. It follows marriage as normally as marriage follows courtship or as autumn follows summer. It is

not a truncation of the process but one of its phases; not the interruption of the dance, but the next figure. We are "taken out of ourselves" by the loved one while she is here. Then comes the tragic figure of the dance in which we must learn to be still taken out of ourselves though the bodily presence is withdrawn, to love the very Her, and not fall back to loving our past, or our memory, or our sorrow, or our relief from sorrow, or our own love.

C. S. Lewis waited a lifetime for Joye. She was with him for just a few years. He then spent the rest of his life waiting for her. But it was worth it. Their love made it all worth it. In fact, the waiting made them cherish their love even more. She was the love of his life, and he would wait an eternity to see her again.

So it is with Christ. We waited for thousands of years for the Messiah to come to us. When he finally came, he was with us for three short years of ministry. Just three years, just a few words, just a brief moment. Then he was gone. And we have been waiting for him ever since.

But why shouldn't we wait for the greatest act of God's love? Do we really expect that something so cosmic, so incredible would happen every day? The very fact that we must wait an eternity to see Christ again—that is further proof of God's handiwork. In our waiting, God molds us in the Divine image. In our waiting, God is asking us to deepen our love for Christ. In our waiting, God is asking us to enter into one of the most profound stages of love.

How to Use this Book

This book is designed to be used during the Advent season of any calendar year. Follow the Sundays and weekdays in parts one, two, and three, until December 16, and then follow the dates of December 17–24 in part four.

The First Week of Advent

The First Sunday of Advent

*Keep awake therefore, for you do not
know on what day your Lord is coming.*
                                    —Matthew 24:42

On the night my first son was born, my husband and I
drove to the hospital at about ten o'clock. There was a full
moon that night, and the light was incredibly bright. I had
spent the entire day at home, feeling the contractions grow in
strength and power, wondering at the mystery that was already
beginning inside my body. As my labor progressed, we took
long walks. We watched our favorite Disney movies. We
played beautiful music and cried together. By ten o'clock, I
knew it was time. The pain was overwhelming, and something
miraculous was about to happen.

As we drove those few miles to the hospital, I looked out
the window at the moon. At that moment, I was fully awake. I
felt the presence of something much greater than myself. I knew

that what was about to happen was out of my hands. I was a creature about to enter a timeless dance that had been initiated by God at the beginning of creation. This was the dance of life itself, and everything in my world was about to change.

I believe that every human being is blessed with such moments, moments when we are truly awake. Perhaps we witness a startling sunset and know beauty as we never have before. Perhaps we wrap our arms around another person as they cry and find our hearts pierced by compassion as never before. Or maybe scales fall from our eyes, and we realize that we have fallen in love. These moments differ radically for each one of us. They are sacred moments. When we find ourselves awake and aware, as God intended us to be, we span the chasm between the worlds of *chronos* and *kairos,* between time and eternity.

As Americans, we spend most of our days in a daze. It is almost as if we were half-asleep. We are so busy, managing packed schedules while entertaining the same repetitious thoughts: *When is my next appointment? Did I pay the bills on time? What's for dinner? Do I need to do the laundry?* If we are not careful, we can spend years of our lives this way. And then we exclaim, "Doesn't time fly?".

But God did not intend for us to go through life this way. God intended for us to be awake. "Keep awake," Jesus instructs, "for the Son of Man comes at an unexpected hour." Jesus is telling us that the quality of our awareness is immensely important. We are asked to open our eyes and recognize the presence of God in our world, in our lives. In fact, Jesus suggests that if we don't stay awake and aware, we could miss the coming of Christ. Our awareness is directly related to our salvation.

In the midst of crazy lives, how can we cultivate this kind of awareness? We cannot have babies every day. Moments of infinite tenderness or beauty don't pop up every day. How can we open our eyes? How can we stay awake?

If we are to keep awake, then we must begin to consider the presence of the Holy in of our daily lives: in a traffic jam, a phone conversation, a search for lost keys. Waking up is a discipline that Buddhists practice regularly. Sit still when you can. Feel your breath. Be aware of your body. Practice opening your eyes to whatever is around you. Remind yourself, from time to time, that life could end in the next moment, the next day. Remind yourself that God has made that purple flower especially for you to see. And God *wants* you to see it: to see it and be awake to its beauty and presence here on earth.

How will the Son of Man come? No one knows but the Father. The Messiah does not make appointments. Instead, Christ breaks into our lives in the strangest ways and at the strangest times—sometimes subtly, sometimes boldly. As we practice being aware of the presence of the Holy in our lives, we will find that it has been there all along.

To Ponder in Prayer

Are we sleeping through life? Well, that's a lot like eating a chocolate praline during a busy meeting and not even tasting it. It's like finding the love of your life and then sleeping soundly as he or she sings outside your window. Today, be awake.

Monday in Week 1

Jesus' words about the centurion:
"[I]n no one in Israel have I found such faith."

—Matthew 8:10

After I graduated from seminary, my husband and I took the trip of a lifetime. We went to Israel–Palestine for almost an entire month. With nothing but backpacks full of clothing, we trekked in the Sinai desert with a Bedouin guide. We went to Jerusalem and the Temple Mount. We walked in the steps of Jesus throughout the Galilee, and my understanding of Scripture was forever changed.

To go to Bethlehem, one has to pass through what is called "no-man's-land"—the zone that serves as a barrier between Israel and areas in which the Palestinian people are living. I was afraid of walking across that silent zone, but I wanted to see the spot where Jesus was born. It was a blazing summer day. We walked slowly from the checkpoint where the Israeli soldiers stood watching us with machine guns. There was deafening silence as we crossed to the Palestinian side. It felt like we were walking through hatred itself. Judgment and fear were almost palpable. I had never seen such hatred between people as I saw in Jerusalem—and this was the Holy Land, the land where God has revealed the Divine self in so many ways.

I'll never forget that walk through no-man's-land. It was not very long, but it seemed to take an eternity. We were caught in the frozen silence of hatred. I could hear myself breathe. It was time outside of time, and I found myself praying that one day zones of hatred like this one would cease to exist.

Isaiah prophesied that when the Messiah comes, nation will not rise up against nation. Weapons will be transformed into gardening tools to harvest the land and feed the hungry. The sword will become a plowshare, the spear a pruning hook. Imagine it. What if, whenever we found ourselves at an impasse on issues of morality, ethnicity, or religion, we simply changed our focus? What if we fed the hungry instead of our hatred? What if we planted crops instead of controversy? Could there ever be such a day?

In this age of ethnic cleansing and religious warring, there is a great temptation to see our enemies and those who wish us harm as evil or barbaric. In a time when technology seems to threaten the core of religious values, it is all too easy to become defensive about our faith, to claim that we alone hold the keys to the mysteries of salvation. It is this kind of judgment and hatred that led Islamic extremists to destroy the World Trade Center. It is this kind of hatred that leads to genocide, ethnic cleansing, and a world of fear.

Jesus was not afraid. He was not afraid to look deep into the heart of the stranger, the heart of the oppressor. Jesus listened to a Centurion, a Roman soldier. Centurions were officers in charge of one hundred Roman soldiers. They were the military police force of the day, occupying the land of the Jews. They were the oppressors, the enemy, and yet Jesus enters into a remarkable conversation with this individual.

The Centurion, like so many others, comes to Jesus out of need. His servant is suffering, and he is desperate. It is desperation that drives this soldier of the mightiest empire on earth to cross the boundaries of ethnicity, religion, and class to make a request of an itinerant Jewish teacher. When Jesus volunteers to come to his house, the Centurion refuses with this most cherished verse: "Lord, I am not worthy to have you come under my roof; but only speak the word and my servant will be healed" (Matthew 8:8).

Here the Centurion reveals that he understands who Jesus really is. While the disciples struggle to comprehend their leader, it is this soldier who catches a glimpse of the majesty of Christ. And he wasn't even a Jew.

Who are we to determine the faith of others? Who are we to judge the heart of another person? Is Christianity really something to be possessed—a set of precepts that save those who swallow them and doom those who do not? Christianity is not a badge to be worn. It is not a ticket to salvation. It is a way to lay the groundwork for a relationship with God.

To Ponder in Prayer

What qualities will enable us to recognize Christ? Scripture gives us no assurance that Christians will recognize the Second Coming ahead of other people. Recognition of the Holy is far more mysterious than that. It has to do with the substance of the soul, the openness of the heart. We must be willing to entertain the possibility that our enemies may recognize God before we do. We must acknowledge that likelihood. Maybe then, instead of casting stones or judgments, we will be able to pull out our gardening tools.

Tuesday in Week 1

*...the earth will be full of the knowledge of the Lord
as the waters cover the sea.*

—Isaiah 11:9

A young couple comes to our church. They are having a child. And though they have thought of God before, read spiritual books, and discussed philosophy and theology over coffee in college, they have never really made their relationship with God a priority until this moment. Now a new life is taking form and shape in their minds as the wife's belly begins to grow. For the first time, they see themselves as parents, teachers. And they feel lost. As the child begins to kick in the mother's belly, the expecting parents realize that they don't know how to raise a child. How will they teach this child to be good? How will they bring meaning into the life of this little one? How will they explain the unique character of this child, the fact that God has given it a personality all its own?

Reaching for answers, the new mother and father begin their search for God.

They come to our church, an Episcopal church, on the recommendation of a friend. The wife was raised Methodist, the husband Catholic, so the Episcopal Church seems like the most sensible choice, straddling their two worlds. They attend services for awhile, sitting in the back. The congregation welcomes them, brings gifts to their house for the baby. Their child, a baby girl, is born healthy. She is baptized and both her parents cry throughout the service. But the mother continues to work nights while the father attends graduate school. They are tired, and they often miss church.

After not seeing them for a few months, I write a note. The mother calls full of tears. She explains that they got swept up in a fundamentalist church on the invitation of a friend. At first, they were so excited. The music was powerful, and the people called them every week to be sure that they got to church. They were quickly incorporated into a Bible study group. They read their Bible every night in preparation for Sunday, and they felt so good about themselves.

But then things began to get complicated. The Bible study group told them that both of their sets of grandparents most certainly were going to hell. They told these young parents that they must be saved immediately, and if their relatives were not saved, they would be damned. Soon the couple found themselves angry, confused, and frightened. They stopped going to church. They slept late on Sundays. They put away their Bibles.

"Can we come back?" the young mother asks through her tears. "Are you mad at us? We wanted a place that would give us all the answers. It seemed so comforting, so easy to be told what to do, how to believe. But when the answers came, I began to appreciate the Episcopal Church. How brave you are to admit that some things are a mystery."

I wish that I could give people solid answers to all of their questions about God. I wish I could tell them exactly why their children die, why their loved ones fall ill, why pain comes to all of us. Though I can point again and again to Scripture, though I can assure people over and over about the magnitude of God's love, I cannot give them all the answers. I don't know the answers myself.

Until Christ comes again, we are left not having all the answers. God has told us only what we need to know now. There is so much that is left unsaid, so much that is unclear. Until that time when "the earth will be full of the knowledge of the Lord as the waters cover the sea," until that time when understanding sweeps over us like a wave crashing upon the dry beach, we will remain ever thirsty for the Holy One.

At this point in our lives, it is important as Christians to admit that we do *not* have all the answers. We are not meant to know everything because Christ has not yet come. The plan of salvation has not yet been fully revealed. When we

admit that we do not know everything, we acknowledge not
only our humanity but the fact that we are a people who will
wait for the culmination of God's plan. We wait for God to
answer those questions that, at the present moment, cannot
be adequately answered.

So we live in the questions themselves, waiting for God
to reveal the Word to us, waiting for Truth to illumine the dark
corners of our minds. This is not instantly gratifying. It does
not sell well in today's market. The idea of mystery is not at-
tractive to the mind that craves security and comfort. But it is
the way of the honest heart, the soul who is not afraid to live
in a period of waiting, to let the emptiness exist.

To Ponder in Prayer

The mystery of God is essential to our lives as Christians. It
is vital that we constantly remind ourselves just how small our
brains are, just how incapable we are of fully answering the
most difficult existential questions. We are human beings, and
we are incomplete without God. God alone can provide all
the answers. Hunger for those answers, and remember that
one day they will be revealed. One day, knowledge will wash
over us like the waves of the sea.

Wednesday in Week 1

On this mountain the Lord of hosts will make for all peoples
a feast of rich food, a feast of well-aged wines,
of rich food filled with marrow, of well-aged wines strained clear.
—Isaiah 25:6

I t's amazing to think about all the changes that have occurred in the past century. We have gone from the horse-drawn carriage to vehicles that can travel over 100 miles an hour. We now can launch ourselves into outer space. We can speak to one another across continents. We can exchange information so fast that there is no end to the knowledge that a person can pursue in her or his own home while seated in front of a computer screen.

No wonder they call this age the Age of Anxiety. It's so hard to keep up with the changes. Some older folks just refuse to do so. One such man, a member of our diocesan council, simply refuses to use e-mail, even though virtually all of our communication now happens that way. "I'm retired," he says. "I'm entitled to resist change."

I once served in a parish located in a small town called Boiling Springs. What used to be a rural area soon became rapidly growing suburbia. When people would ask me how long I had served in the church, I liked to tell them that I had arrived just before the Walmart. It was an easy point of reference. The road where the church sat became one big shopping strip, from Spartanburg to the lake, right before our very eyes. We had a beauty shop that was built on one side of us and, just beyond that, a pecan orchard with a donkey grazing. One of the reasons I had moved to Boiling Springs was to escape from the pressure of the big city. But the city was moving in on us. There was even some traffic around the junior high school in the mornings. I hear from friends there that they now have bona fide traffic jams in Boiling Springs.

Our diets have changed, too. Today, Americans spend more money on fast food than we do on higher education. Many Americans eat out multiple times a week. In our rush to make the next appointment, we jog by McDonald's and pick up two Happy Meals for our kids and a fish sandwich for ourselves. We are used to food that is produced for us in an instant, all wrapped in colorful boxes and paper. If Daniel Boone walked into a supermarket, it might take him awhile to realize that it was food that was being sold. It is so well packaged that it could be just about anything. Everything is so well preserved that there are very few aromas or smells, even in a "Super Walmart." And food is in abundance. When a friend of mine from Russia came to visit the United States about six years ago, she walked into the local supermarket and burst into tears. She had never seen so much food in her life.

All this abundance makes it hard for us to understand the depth and meaning of Isaiah's vision of a banquet in God's Kingdom. To fully understand Isaiah's message, we must be aware of the many places in this world where people really are hungry. We must imagine what life is like in countries today where food is grown locally, cultivated, and eaten. In many countries there is no refrigeration, no canning or preservatives. Food is harvested and eaten shortly thereafter. People who live this way know that food is life itself. Without food people die. One can see the connection. For people who are hungry, there is no greater assurance of continuing life than a table set with plenty of food.

For the hungry of Isaiah's time, heaven was a place with abundant food. In that place where God grants salvation, there would be a table set with a banquet. There would be rich food, fine wine. In the banquet that never ends, God would grant us eternal life.

Do you remember, as a child, smelling dinner as it baked in the oven? Do you remember waiting while your stomach growled, knowing that at some point that dish would be taken out of the oven, steaming hot, and placed on the table? Were you ever blessed enough to know that feeling—the feeling of waiting for a good meal?

To this day, my greatest joy is eating with my family. Even when we sit down to something as simple as macaroni and cheese: when we join hands and thank God, I know that the four of us are alive, that we are together, and that we are nourished. The nourishment that is provided by that food assures me that life will continue. I look up from our meal to the faces of my loved ones, and I catch a glimpse of the Kingdom.

To Ponder in Prayer

Imagine eternal life as a banquet filled with food, a place where our deepest hunger is satisfied. Can you imagine dinner with God? The smell, the taste? God would call us all to the table. "Welcome. Come and eat," the Holy One might say. That is what we anticipate in the sacrament of Holy Eucharist. That meal, that life, that communion.

Thursday in Week 1

Everyone who hears these words of mine and acts on them will be like a wise man who built his house on rock. The rain fell, the floods came, and the winds blew and beat on that house, but it did not fall, because it had been founded on rock. And everyone who hears these words of mine and does not act on them will be like a foolish man who built his house on sand. The rain fell, and the floods came, and the winds blew and beat against that house, and it fell—and great was its fall!

—Matthew 7:24–27

My sons love the old Disney video of the three pigs. The plump little pigs dance around in circles singing "Who's afraid of the big bad wolf?" over and over again. As we all know, two of the pigs made houses that would not stand up to the wolf's ferocious breath. It is not explained why one pig built a house of straw and the other built a house of sticks. Were they aiming for cheap material? Were they actually foolish enough to believe that their houses would stand up? Who knows? They both end up running to their practical third brother, who not only protects his siblings in his brick house but burns the wolf in a hot cauldron when he tries to climb down the chimney.

At least once a week, a parishioner approaches me to apologize for not making it to church on Sunday. People seem guilt-ridden by their absence. But they do not need to feel guilty. If they looked deeper inside themselves, most of them would realize that they actually missed being in church—that it was they who needed God, not God that needed them. One woman expressed it this way: "My week just doesn't seem to go right if I miss church." Another man, who was baptized as an adult, explained to me that now that he is attending church, he feels as though he is walking on solid ground.

In this world, the winds of change seem to blow from out of nowhere. We never know what the next day, the next hour will hold. One year ago, a woman in my parish was walking with her two sons along a country road. A drunk driver came speeding around a curve and hit her fourteen-year-old son. Her son was killed instantly, right in front of her eyes. Not only did she have to witness the death of her child, but she had to go to court some eight months later and testify as a witness in a case against the driver. There was evidence of cocaine, marijuana, and alcohol in his urine, and yet he acted as if he were annoyed to be there in that courtroom. He acted as if he shouldn't be bothered with all this, that he had done nothing wrong. He might as well have hit a tree.

Through the horror of this event, this woman held onto her faith, even though her house was shaken. She would come into my office each week and cry for an hour. Neither of us could shake off the terrifying reality of her son's death. I could give her no reasons for why this had happened. I could only assure her that this tragedy was not God's will but the result of another human being's actions—a human being who chose to drink and drive.

Though her pain was as acute as any I have seen, this woman's house stood. She was able to testify to the truth of the event before a jury without fainting or breaking down. She was able to give her son over to the hands of a loving God, who she believed would take care of him and of her. She is alive today. She is a woman of great courage and faith. And when people ask her about her younger son, she tells them that he lives in heaven.

What would this woman have done had she not built her house on the rock of Christ? I don't know if she could have survived such a tidal wave. Following the teachings of Jesus— praying, giving, forgiving others—prepares a soul for salvation. To refrain from following Jesus' instructions is to neglect making the most important long-term investment of a lifetime. It is like building a house that's destined to fall.

To Ponder in Prayer

Why do we spend our time, our money, our lives building houses of straw and sticks? Why do we make our careers our top priority? Why do we save all of our money without any thought of giving back to God? Why do we vacation and travel, but rarely find the time to set foot in church? Silly little pigs we are.

Friday in Week 1

As Jesus went on from there, two blind men followed him, crying loudly, "Have mercy on us, Son of David!" When he entered the house, the blind men came to him; and Jesus said to them, "Do you believe that I am able to do this?" They said to him, "Yes, Lord." Then he touched their eyes and said, "According to your faith let it be done to you." And their eyes were opened. Then Jesus sternly ordered them, "See that no one knows of this." But they went away and spread the news about him throughout the district. —Matthew 9:27–31

The youth group at our church loves to play the game of trust. We all join hands and close our eyes. The person in the very front of the line is the only one allowed to keep her eyes open. She then leads the group all over the building, even outside.

Until I had played this game with them, I never realized how frightening it is to not see. Common sounds become heightened and startle us. The ground under our feet does not feel quite so solid. We are more aware of smells, and we can sense motion around us. The game forces us to trust one another, to depend on the hand ahead to guide us and the one behind to steady us along the path.

Of course, I do not really know what it is like to be blind, to have never seen. Conversely, I don't think that anyone could explain what it means to see to someone who has been deprived entirely of that sense from birth. How could you explain the lived experience of sight to a person who had no frame of reference, who cannot distinguish light from darkness? It would be impossible.

It strikes me that faith is a good deal like that trust walk. We cannot see God. We cannot meet and talk to Jesus in person. Instead we must rely on the stories of Scripture, the words of those who have gone ahead of us, the words of the ones who saw him, touched him, talked to him. We are asked to join hands and walk what early Christians called "the Way" without seeing the road before us. We are blind to our destination, blind to our future. We trust that Christ has walked ahead of us and will shepherd us over the bridge that leads from this life into the next.

It seems to me that this is what the Apostolic Succession is all about. All that laying on of hands: from Peter to a disciple, to a bishop, to another bishop, and so on down the line. Christians have intentionally initiated one another into the Church through physical touch. If we are confirmed into the Episcopal Church, the bishop lays his or her hands on us, and we are linked all the way back to the apostles. We are holding onto each other, trusting that the one ahead of us has held the hand of the one in front of him or her, and so on . . . all the way back to Jesus. In our blindness, we cannot see God. But we can trust the touch of the one in front of us.

I wonder what it was like for these two blind men when Jesus opened their eyes. They must have seen a blur of color. They could not have had the knowledge to discern what it was that they were seeing. They must have been overwhelmed. I cannot imagine waking to another sense all at once. I can only liken it to a baby who emerges from her mother's womb: though unable to discern the shape of faces, she still stares at light and patterns with an intensity that goes beyond curiosity.

But for Jesus, the acquisition of sight was not the important issue—he was concerned with the faith of these two men. Before healing them, he asked if indeed they believed in his capacity to heal. He wanted to foster their faith in him, their faith in God.

Emerging from this life into the next must be like the experience of the blind men. Jesus will open our eyes to senses that we have never known, to experiences that we could never have imagined. I'm sure that we can no more understand the nature of heaven than one who is blind can understand the nature of light. We must simply trust in the One who walks ahead of us, trust that he will open our eyes when the time is right.

To Ponder in Prayer

A woman in the parish I serve had a dream a few years ago. In the dream, she saw the sky tear just a bit. Through the rip in the atmosphere, she could catch a glimpse of heaven. She came into my office the next morning with tears in her eyes. "I cannot describe it," she said. "There were colors there. Colors more vibrant, more real than anything that I have ever seen. They made everything here seem like it exists in black, white, and gray. They were *colors....*"

And their eyes were opened. One day our eyes will be opened too....

Saturday in Week 1

Though the Lord may give you the bread of adversity and the water of affliction, yet your Teacher will not hide himself anymore, but your eyes shall see your Teacher. And when you turn to the right or when you turn to the left, your ears shall hear a word behind you, saying, "This is the way; walk in it."

—Isaiah 30: 20–21

Some people like change and others do not. Some people can't wait for the latest advance in technology, and others wish that things would slow down. But regardless of whether we like change or it scares us to death, it comes. It's constant. Change just keeps on coming. It's part of life—especially life in the twenty-first century. We live in a time of massive cultural transition. The growth spurt in technology we have witnessed in this century leaves us contending with a new high-speed world, and we are not yet sure how to change our thinking to fit this new era.

The people of Jesus' day were also living in a time of transition. They saw the Messiah himself come, and after his resurrection and ascension, it was up to them to spread the news. They had to change their minds about everything. No longer were they like their ancestors, waiting for the Son of David. Christ had come, and he had taught them a new way of thinking, a new way of believing. Now they had to learn to live as believers.

We like to think that the early Christian movement was a time of great excitement, great joy, oneness in Spirit and contentment. But it was not. From the very beginning, the Church hit problems. Just read the Acts of the Apostles or the letters of Paul. People seemed either to love or hate Paul. Some believed what he taught about Jesus. Others talked behind his back, and still others openly tried to kill him. Often Paul was forced to leave one place and go somewhere else. He didn't even have a home, much less a steady income. This man's life was change itself. And so were the lives of all the early Christians. At first they didn't even call themselves "Christians," but "The People of the Way."

It is comforting to consider Christianity as some kind of set of beliefs or group to which we can belong. We like to think of church as a set of ancient buildings, a compilation of traditions, a set worship service—but these are only the trappings. Life for the true follower of Christ is all about movement and change. Christianity is a path, a way to God.

It is a journey. It is choices and challenges. It is doing your best to move closer to God.

When Jesus was talking with his disciples, he told them that he was the Way, the Truth, and the Life (John 14:6). In other words, life with Christ is not stagnant. If you are comfortable and not moving, then you cannot be following the Way. No, in order to follow the Way, one must move. One must change.

My father-in-law had prostate cancer that eventually moved into his bones. As he neared death he was in pain, on a morphine patch. And I didn't want this change—his death—to happen. More than anything, I wanted to have him around a little longer. He was my mentor and my friend. I just didn't want this change to take place. When I look back on his life, though, I see that it was when he embraced the changes that were of God that he made the greatest impact in his life. Like when he angered so many people around him by marching down Poplar Avenue in Memphis the day after Dr. Martin Luther King, Jr. was shot. People all around him jeered and some even spit at him, but he walked anyway. On that day in Memphis, Don knew that things were changing, and he knew the Way.

Change is the only constant of life. Children grow up, people die. We can't hide from change. But we can choose the path that we travel. We can choose to be dragged unwillingly, or we can walk the way of Truth and Life.

To Ponder in Prayer

It's hard to look forward and ask yourself where God wants you to go. It means accepting the fact that life continues to move forward with or without you. It means accepting that God is calling us to walk along the Way that leads to eternal life. No wonder the first Christians called their religion "The Way." That's what life in Christ is like: it is movement, it is change, and it is not easy.

The Second Week of Advent

The Second Sunday of Advent

In those days John the Baptist
appeared in the wilderness of Judea....
—Matthew 3:1

John the baptizer appeared in the wilderness....
—Mark 1:4

[T]he word of God came to John
son of Zechariah in the wilderness....
—Luke 3:2

According to the Gospel of Luke, John was the son of Zechariah, a priest of the temple. Zechariah was among the few privileged religious leaders who were allowed to enter the inner sanctum of the temple. Not only was Zechariah part of the religious establishment, he was one of the elite. He was given inside access to God. The Jews of his day would have considered Zechariah as one who had laid eyes on God. His words and actions would bear an authority far beyond that of the average community member. There was no higher status within Judaism.

Zechariah's only son would have received the best education in Judaism. He would have been spoon-fed the Torah from a young age. He would have been cared for with great attention. After all, he was the son of a High Priest. No doubt John would have been accepted into the Harvard of his day.

As with Jesus, there are many gaps in our knowledge of the life of John. We hear about his birth and then we see him, years later, hanging out as a recluse in the wilderness. What happened? There is a disconnect between the privileged birth of the child and the idiosyncratic life of the adult. If we are to take the Lucan account at face value, then we must assume that John separated himself from his upbringing and willingly chose the wilderness.

Why would a child of such privilege, a child born into such authority, give up the life that has been handed to him on a silver platter? Why leave all that behind? John, quite literally, traded in the life of an elite Jew for the life of a homeless man.

So driven by the prophecy that consumed him, John evidently was willing to sever all ties to his inherited life. He separated himself from every part of Jewish tradition and custom. He left his life behind and struck out alone.

I believe that John's self-segregation was born of the fact that he knew that his message was wholly new. He knew that there was something out there for which he must give his life. He needed with such intensity to listen to this new message that he left everything else behind. His message was so different, so radical, that he could not remain in traditional life. He had to leave everything else behind just to listen.

John's radicalness, his solitude, his differentness also caused people to listen to him with new ears. This was not a priest preaching to them from the steps of the temple, surrounded by years of architecture and custom. No, this man had struck out to do something totally different. This man was going to say something that never had been said before. He was going to entertain ideas that never had been conceived of, thoughts that never had been considered. Those who heard John had to travel out of their ordinary lives, out of their comfort zones, to hear something wholly new.

An original thought is difficult to find these days. To really say something new in my sermons, I often must leave my life behind for awhile. Go outside, sit in silence, ache for a moment as I wait for God to fill the void. The voice of originality cannot be heard amidst the din of our busy lives. But God often waits patiently for us to set routine aside so we can hear the unique word of the Holy Spirit.

John was courageous. He was willing to leave his privileged life behind and enter into the dirty, scary, risky life of a prophet. He had the courage to enter the emptiness and entertain a new thought.

There are many prophets that I would place in the company of John the Baptizer. They are those who risked rejection, loneliness, and ostracism for the originality of a truly new idea: Einstein, Mozart, Bach, Picasso . . . you name the rest. They are the cornerstones of human development. For the voice of God always will reveal itself to those who are willing to enter the threatening possibility of emptiness.

To Ponder in Prayer

Do I have the courage to face emptiness and listen for God's original will for my life?

Monday in Week 2

Strengthen the weak hands,
and make firm the feeble knees.
Say to those who are of a fearful heart,
"Be strong, do not fear!
Here is your God.
He will come with vengeance,
with terrible recompense.
He will come and save you."

—Isaiah 35:3–4

Working as a priest in a parish is a study in human nature. The longer that I minister to people, the more I realize that fear is a fundamental part of human nature. Especially in the face of death and loss, fear can be overwhelming.

At the bedside of a loved one who is dying, people revert to a kind of infancy. The feeling of helplessness that they experience is often more than they can stand. Grief after the death of a loved one can be so acute as to cause illness. I knew a man who died of grief. He simply could not live without his wife. His heart stopped.

Often families who lose a loved one need very basic care around the time of the funeral. They cannot hear much. Words are virtually useless. Their fear and grief can become so acute, so deep, that they are reduced to a state that is beyond words, a state that defies explanation. Only physical touch can curb their loneliness. A hand held, the brush of a cheek: these can be consoling. People are often relieved to see that I have tissues waiting in my office. The presence of this little box of tissues gives them permission to cry. Sometimes a person cannot make it through the funeral service without being held. I often ask friends and family to provide this care. They have permission to cry and hold one another; sometimes it is absolutely necessary.

Last week, a man suffering from the early stages of Alzheimer's stood at the edge of his wife's grave, waiting as they lowered the casket into the ground. Most families leave for this last and most final stage of the burial. I let families know that they can leave, but I often stay and bless the body as it descends into the earth. This man was adamant in his desire to stay. "Oh," he kept saying as they lowered the casket into the ground. "Oh, no," he kept repeating, as the reality of his loss hit him over and over again with the merciless repetition of the Alzheimer's mind. The fake grass had been pulled away; one could see the dirt below along with the chains and pulleys used to lower that heavy box into the ground. He would look around, see the beautiful blue sky, and then turn to the open grave and realize the reality of his loss once more. No one could make him move from that place. Helpless, he just stood there saying "Oh!" while his daughter and I held him.

After the casket reached the bottom of the pit, this man looked at me. With an intensity in his eyes that I will never forget, he asked, "Is she in heaven now?" And I nodded. He began to gather roses from the spray. "I will dry these and keep them," he said.

It is no wonder to me that God had to become enfleshed in human form to comfort us. There is simply no other way to do it. Words are insufficient when someone dies. Only the presence and touch of another human being can comfort those who grieve. Jesus had to walk with us, touch us, be with us. It was the only way.

To Ponder in Prayer

Picture how Christ came to us, how he cried with Mary and Martha at the death of their brother. Christ came once, and Christ will come again to help us move beyond our fear and into a new world of freedom.

Tuesday in Week 2

Jesus said, "What do you think? If a shepherd has a hundred sheep, and one of them has gone astray, does he not leave the ninety-nine on the mountains and go in search of the one that went astray? And if he finds it, truly I tell you, he rejoices over it more than over the ninety-nine that never went astray. So it is not the will of your Father in heaven that one of these little ones should be lost." —Matthew 18:10-14

Like most Christian churches, we stage a Christmas pageant every year. Two years ago, the director and I decided to let our two- and three-year-olds be in the pageant. But how to cast them? Obviously, they could not sit still for more than two seconds. There was no way to prevent them from wandering all over the congregation. Then it hit me. Sheep. We could cast them as sheep. Then if they wandered, it would be in character. So we dressed all these little ones in sheep's costumes, complete with fuzzy ears. We had white, black, and gray sheep. And they wandered everywhere that Sunday. They stole the show.

Last year during our summer festival, my three-year-old son Luke was lost. Because our church is smaller, I was used to him disappearing on Sundays. It was not uncommon to find him being held by a parishioner and fed a cookie. I did not worry about him. I knew that if he was out of my sight, he was being well taken care of.

But our summer festival was different. We had hundreds of people all over the church grounds. There were children's rides, games, food, crafts. Everyone was working, and no one was watching Luke. I'll never forget the white look on my husband J. D.'s face as he ran up to me. "Do you have Luke?" he asked. I had not seen Luke in over half an hour.

We scoured the church grounds, and my panic rose to an intensity that I had never felt before. Abductions were all over the news, in the papers. Where was my son? All the noises of the celebration around me fell silent. I could only hear my heart pounding against my chest as I ran around searching. Thoughts began to enter my head: *What would I do without him? What would I do if he were taken from me? Could I even survive? He would be helpless at three, unable to defend himself. Oh, God, let him be safe,* I prayed. *Let me find him.*

The panic and wrenching fear that I felt is not unlike the pain that God must feel when we run away from the Divine presence. We are as much a part of God as our offspring are a part of us. God will not be satisfied until all people have returned home, until the whole creation is reconciled. God searches for us with an intensity that I believe we find overwhelming.

In those moments when Luke was missing, I was actively searching for him. I was running around frantically, looking everywhere that I could think of. And yet at the same time, I was waiting. I was waiting and praying for Luke to appear. I was waiting for his whereabouts to be revealed.

Just because God does not force us into the Divine presence does not mean that God does not actively seek us. I do not believe that God passively sits up in heaven waiting for us to climb up there somehow. No, God searches for us. If we just hold still long enough, God will find us. If we look for God, we may meet even sooner. But Jesus is clear with us that the Shepherd actively looks for the missing sheep. When we wander, God does not sit still and wait for us to return. God seeks us out.

Countless times people have come to my office to tell me that they are tired of running from God. So many of us run, and yet we find that we cannot avoid the presence of the Holy forever. God will find us.

Luke had hidden himself in a corner of the sanctuary. I guess that he was tired of the crowds and needed some quiet time. He sat there playing with his trains, while we urgently searched. When we found him, my breath returned. For the rest of the day and many days that followed, I gave thanks. Even to this day, I can remember that feeling of panic. I am so thankful to have him with me.

To Ponder in Prayer

It's scary to think that God might be looking for us. Scary to think that our souls might matter so much to God that God might search for us with that same intensity that we would search for our children. It's scary because it means that our actions matter to God. It means that we do not live just for ourselves. It means that God's love is active. There is a love out there that will pursue us and not let us go.

Wednesday in Week 2

Come to me, all you that are weary and are carrying heavy burdens, and I will give you rest. Take my yoke upon you, and learn from me; for I am gentle and humble in heart, and you will find rest for your souls. For my yoke is easy, and my burden is light.
        —Matthew 11:28–30

Every time I celebrate the Eucharist, I place a stole over my shoulders. My spiritual director wove my stoles on her loom: beautiful, intricate weavings of green, white, gold, purple, and red threads. I kiss the cross in the middle of the long piece of woven fabric and place the stole over my shoulders. All priests must wear a stole when we celebrate the Eucharist. The stole signifies the burden of Christ.

  Last year, I came to know a man who had battled lifelong depression. After years of pain and struggle, he had sought medical treatment. Shock therapy, medications, and psychoanalysis: all three helped him learn to live again. He worked hard on the reasons for his depression and sought to cure himself in every way possible. Rarely had I seen such drive to become well. But after all his work, something was still missing. At times, he found himself slipping back into gloom. He had a steady job, life seemed good on every level, but he could not seem to relinquish the temptation to give in to his "lows."

While coming to church, he began to realize something. He had not taken the final step towards health: he had not yet taken on the burden of Christ. He needed to somehow use his pain, his lifelong struggle, as a source of ministry. He needed to take on Christ's struggle and give himself to God in service of others.

After starting a support group and taking communion regularly to the sick and shut-in, he began to smile, to really smile.

I have seen it time and time again. It is not enough for us simply to unload our burdens in therapy and seek happiness. We will never find true wholeness until we do what is counterintuitive, until we take on the burden of Christ. It is in learning to care for others that the greatest joy is to be found. But it's hard to believe Jesus' words: that his yoke is easy and his burden is light. Instead we spend so much of our lives convinced that happiness is just beyond the next hurdle. If only we earn more money, buy that new car, or go on that perfect vacation, then we would find happiness. After all, that's what the commercials tell us.

Strange that it is in taking on a burden that we find fulfillment. One would not think that it would be so. But Jesus knew what he was talking about. When we place that yoke of service to God on our shoulders, God gives us rest. *Rest for our souls,* that's what Jesus promises. Rest from the torment of self-absorption, rest from endless searching for that perfect product that will make us complete, rest from the need to constantly do well and be liked. The rest that we all have been seeking for the entirety of our lives.

Even before I could articulate any of this—before seminary, before ordination, I always went to see a lonely elderly lady who lived in a nearby nursing home when I felt low. Somehow, in doing something for her, I was healed. In bringing her communion, I found peace. It makes no sense at all, no sense at all.

To Ponder in Prayer

Here is one of the best kept secrets of the Christian world: if you take on Christ's priorities, if you take on his cares and concerns, you will find yourself at peace. For it is in service that we find ourselves healed. God lifts us out of the mire of self-absorption and into the life of ministry.

Thursday in Week 2

Every day will I bless you,
and praise your name forever and ever.
— Psalm 145:2

There are three windows beside my bed. They reach from the floor to the ceiling. Outside there is a pond, and trees flank the water. The sun rises behind that pond. Every morning, sunlight filters in, dancing its reflections off the water, through the leaves, and into my room.

Mornings are crazy with two toddlers in the house. I usually awake to the call of "Mama!" from Jacob, my two-year-old, who often wakes just as the sun is beginning to rise. My husband and I then go about our morning procrastination ritual. Whose turn is it to get up first, anyway?

This morning, there was a gorgeous southern fog over the pond. In a spontaneous act of generosity, J. D. got up first, despite his cold. I lay there in a cherished moment of peace. *Every day will I bless you, and praise your name forever and ever.* The psalmist wrote these words thousands of years ago. And even today, I cannot say it better. There are days when I feel my heart burst within me. When the sun rises, I find that I must praise the One who made the miracle of its ascent into the sky.

I wish that I could feel this kind of spontaneous devotion every morning without exception. This is prayer at its best: the heart full of love, the beauty of creation before me, time to soak it all in. But many mornings are not like this. I often drag myself out of bed and into the world of Batman and Robin before my mind is even functioning. And the nights are often not much better. After the kids are finally asleep, the last story is read and songs are sung, often I will need to phone a parishioner who is ill, check my answering machine at work, pay bills. I will plop myself down on the floor in front of my icon of Christ and pray for some sense of God's presence, but sometimes all that I feel is tired and anxious.

Should I pray to God even when I don't feel like it? Is it like jogging? Do I simply need to force myself to pray every day at a certain hour, rain or shine, babies crying or quiet? How does one balance spontaneity with discipline in the life of prayer?

This is the struggle of all who seek to come to know God. How and when do you pray? Is there a right time and a wrong time? Will God forgive me if I just go to bed tonight instead of saying evening prayer? How does one decide? How can I make my soul ready for the coming of Christ?

If we truly believe that the purpose of life is to prepare ourselves for God's kingdom, then we must foster that relationship. Our relationship with God is, quite simply, the most important relationship in our lives. And just as I must take time to go on dates with my husband for the good of my marriage, so must I take time to foster my relationship with God. I must make time every day.

But the manner in which I spend time with God can vary. Every day I will bless God, but sometimes that will be by sitting down with Scripture. Sometimes, it will mean that I meditate before my icon. Sometimes I will sing, sometimes I will form words to speak to God. Sometimes I will sit in silence while my mind wanders. But I must always give it time. Every day, in some fashion, I must follow the example of the psalmist and praise God.

To Ponder in Prayer

"How do I find the time for prayer?" people ask me. "How can I make it a priority?" It should be *the* priority. We spend time buying life insurance policies, putting money away for retirement. Isn't eternal life worth an investment of time? To me, it's a no-brainer. By comparison, everything else is a waste of time.

Friday in Week 2

For John came neither eating nor drinking, and they say, "He has a demon"; the Son of Man came eating and drinking, and they say, "Look, a glutton and a drunkard, a friend of tax collectors and sinners!" Yet wisdom is vindicated by her deeds.

—Matthew 11: 18–19

They did not recognize John. They thought that he was strange. They thought he acted weird. They thought that he had a demon. Why in the world would someone fast as much as he did? Why would someone wear such strange clothes?

Then Jesus came, eating and drinking, and they thought him too relaxed, too greedy. Both the Incarnation of God and God's greatest prophet were missed simply because they did not fit the bill. People got caught up in habits and details. They got stuck in criticism of the minutia that so consumed their lives, in rules broken and traditions brushed aside. And they lost out. The majority of women and men who saw these two men firsthand failed to recognize them. They missed the hand of God because they were so caught up in the details.

This happens time and time again in the life of a parish. We will be doing God's work: worshiping, feeding the poor, learning about Scripture and building community. Then a tradition will be forgotten or changed. We will decide to move the baptismal font. I will forget to activate the prayer chain for someone's grandmother's surgery, and rage will ensue. Parishioners will leave the community over such things as the color of the walls or a misspoken word. We will focus on the missed detail. We will feel such anger over the rule broken that we fail to recognize God's presence among us, and the devil of division reigns once more.

Jesus was not one for following the rules. He changed everything. He had little respect for social customs or adherences to religious traditions. He was not one to mince words. He called the religious authorities vipers. He named people's sins right to their faces, and still, few were able to recognize who he was. Instead, the majority of those who saw Jesus chose to focus on his idiosyncrasies, and in doing so, they missed his message.

Life in community is a series of psychological and spiritual challenges. You can be sure that someone will push your buttons eventually. But when our buttons are pushed, we must ask ourselves: Is this a dispute over rules, or is God's presence really at issue here? If it is about a tradition of the church, a mistake that was made, or some other customary issue, then is the adherence to this rule so vital that we should divide ourselves from our community?

I suppose that the root of our grievance and criticism is fear, fear of what is different, fear of change, fear of the new, fear of the disturbance of our world. If we let this fear reign in our lives, however, we certainly will miss the coming of Christ. If we *know* God, we must know that Christ won't come in any comfortable or expected way. We can bet that the Holy One will break the rules. I suppose that the only thing we *can* expect is the unexpected.

If we are to anticipate the coming of Christ in spirit and truth, then we must open ourselves to the existence of the unfamiliar, the unexpected. We must learn to see beyond custom and tradition to the message of the one who speaks, to the motivation, the meaning. We must ask ourselves, in every encounter, "Is God trying to tell me something here? If so, what might that message be?"

To Ponder in Prayer

Few things are more threatening to the spiritual life than comfort for its own sake. There is no greater obstacle in the life of a parish than tradition for tradition's sake. "We have *always* done it this way," we say. But God doesn't speak in the language of predictability. God speaks in the language of challenge and of change. How does your own comfort hinder your relationship with God?

Saturday in Week 2

[Jesus] replied, "Elijah is indeed coming and will restore all things; but I tell you that Elijah has already come, and they did not recognize him, but they did to him whatever they pleased. So also the Son of Man is about to suffer at their hands." Then the disciples understood that he was speaking to them about John the Baptist. —Matthew 17:11–13

The longer that I serve as an ordained minister, the lonelier I become. It seems that in order to be a truly effective priest, I must give up the possibility of becoming friends with my parishioners. Friendship with them just doesn't work. Although they may *say* that they want a friend, what they really want is a person of God. They need someone who can put aside their own personal issues and listen. They need someone who can preach the truth of Scripture from the pulpit and not try to please the listeners. They need someone who is not afraid to tell them the truth, even if they do not like the message. People need a priest.

A while ago, I stood in the playground with a couple from my parish. Our children, the same ages exactly, were playing on the swings. The father and I were discussing the life of clergy. His brother was now in seminary, and this had led him to rethink his own relationships with ordained ministers.

"I remember," he said, "years ago, when the pastor at my church made some mistakes. He told us that he was going to leave to accept a position at another church. Then he changed his mind. I was so incensed that this man would be so careless and indecisive. I was furious. I criticized him behind his back. I complained to him in person. He was going through a painful divorce at the time and not once did I ask how he was doing. It's only now, years later, that I realize that I only wanted my needs met. Somehow, because he was clergy, I didn't think of him as a person. I didn't think of the fact that he might have needs, too."

Just a few weeks ago, I was walking in the mall with my husband and our two little boys. I was having a professional photo taken, so I was wearing my black clerical shirt and collar. The teenagers were all about in various groups, posturing and eying each other. They would be looking all around as we walked by when, all of a sudden, their eyes would fix on us: me in my collar, two baby boys in stroller, and a husband who had just shaved his head. The stares were undeniable. "Now I know what it feels like to be Amish," my husband said.

This isolation is not an issue just for clergy. It is an issue for all who seek to follow God in a serious way. A whole-hearted commitment to serve God can isolate a person from the rest of her or his family and friends. I see it in the parish I serve: the more people devote themselves to serving God, the more estranged they become from their old way of life. The more that they tell the truth, the more truly they serve God, the more they become aware of the problems and deficiencies of the rest of the world. The cost of discipleship is a kind of isolation. The more we serve God, the more we exist between two worlds.

The ultimate example of such devotion is found in Jesus and the prophets. Take Elijah. He traveled from place to place, telling people about the will of God. He was chased out of some places and welcomed in others. He cured the sick, even brought a dead child back to life. But this prophecy and miracle-working served to isolate him from his contemporaries. John the Baptist isolated himself in the wilderness and eventually was beheaded. Jesus found himself on the cross.

True devotion threatens the worldly. Effective ministry in this world often leads to a kind of healthy distance. There is love, but there is no longer enmeshment. Like the most effective therapist, a good priest does not burden people with his or her own problems, but is there to listen.

It strikes me that God, when given the opportunity, will not stop until we are utterly devoted. The journey to God is one of continual detachment from this world, even as we serve in the midst of it. And the more we serve God, the more the love of this world just won't satisfy our deepest hunger. We long for the bread of life, and nothing else satisfies.

To Ponder in Prayer

Can you let go of the opinions of others and rely on God?

The Third Week of Advent

The Third Sunday of Advent

They shall see the glory of the Lord,
the majesty of our God.   —Isaiah 35:2

I will rejoice in Jerusalem,
and delight in my people;
no more shall the sound of weeping be heard in it,
or the cry of distress.   —Isaiah 65:19

Do not fear, O Zion;
do not let your hands grow weak.
The Lord, your God, is in your midst.

—Zephaniah 3:16–17

My mother stayed at home with me as a child. Every day I would walk one block from school to our house. I knew to push the button on the pole beside the curb and to wait until the sign said Walk before crossing the street. And every day, without fail, my mother was there to greet me when I got home. Until that one day.

She said that she got caught in traffic. I must have been in kindergarten or first grade. I came home and the door was locked. Panic rose inside, a feeling that I can still recall vividly. I clung to the picket fence in front of our house and cried hard. I thought that the world was coming to an end.

Just as vivid remains the feeling that I experienced when my mother's car pulled into the driveway. The world was righted. I found my balance again and let go of the fence. Things came into focus. I could breathe. And then, later, I got mad.

I don't think that we are fully aware of the depth of our longing for God. We long for the return of the Holy One with the same kind of intensity that a child longs for her mother. But most of us have buried this feeling along with all the other "childish" fears that we instruct ourselves to ignore. "You can't be afraid of the dark anymore," we tell ourselves when the lights go out in our office building late one night. "You're an adult," we remind ourselves. But the truth is that we are afraid. And whether or not we admit it to ourselves, we still get scared, anxious, and uneasy at times. Who wouldn't be afraid? I can't tell you for sure that I will be alive tomorrow, and if I let myself really recognize that reality, I get scared.

Fear not, says Isaiah the prophet. God will come and make things right. God will be here to be seen and touched and heard. You will be able to breathe again, for things will be put in their proper place, and the world will be brought back into focus.

We may not realize how much we have longed for Christ's return until we see Christ face-to-face. We may not realize the extent of our fear and expectation until we are safe in the presence of the Holy One. I imagine that we will look back on this time of waiting and wonder how it was that we held on for so long. We will be amazed at the violence, the fear, the suffering that we had to cope with in our world. We will marvel at the way in which we held on for dear life, trying to do the best that we could, waiting for things to be made right. Just as you and I often look back on difficult periods of our lives in wonder, so will we look back on this time of waiting and marvel at our own strength.

To Ponder in Prayer

To fully understand the comfort that will come with Christ's arrival, we must acknowledge Christ's absence. We must look deep inside at the child within that still longs to be comforted when we are alone, that longs for the kind of companion who never grows tired of us and celebrates our uniqueness. Where are the vacancies in your life? How do you long to be fed? What in your life remains empty? It is okay to suffer, to ponder, to wait. The greater our longing, the greater the relief when Christ comes. Some things can only be made right by the Holy One of God.

Monday in Week 3

The oracle of Balaam son of Beor,
The oracle of the man whose eye is clear,
The oracle of one who hears the words of God,
And knows the knowledge of the Most High....

—Numbers 24:15–16

Sticks and stones may break my bones, but words will never hurt me. This old nursery rhyme is not true. It is a lie. For thousands of years, we have known the power of words.

Very little has changed in the human condition. Three thousand years ago, one man's opinion of another had great impact and implications. The same is true today. What was once called an "oracle" and received from a prophet in ancient Israel, we now call a "diagnosis" or "second opinion." The words of others impact the way that we see ourselves, the way that we live, the way that we die.

The opinions of others are particularly powerful among

the young. Teenagers often define their interests, their
achievements, even their self-worth based on the opinions of
their peers. The effect of peer pressure on teens can be dev-
astating. Just a few weeks ago, a teenager overdosed on drugs
while on the Internet, simply to impress his on-line friends.
"Wow, man," they said, "you sure can do a ton of drugs! Do
more! *More!*" And he died. Where were his values? How
could he succumb so completely to the words of others, to the
words of people he could not even *see?* How could he have
been so impressionable?

We see the effects of human opinion in the media. Just
look at the lives of our celebrities. Under the microscope of
intense public scrutiny, the divorce rate among celebrities is
sky-high. Often their relationships simply cannot tolerate the
rumors that surround their every move. Is she having an af-
fair? Is he satisfied? Who can withstand such words? It's no
wonder that so many relationships break down, that drug use
is rampant, that people who seem so beautiful on the outside
are hurting so badly on the inside.

Balaam the prophet was asked to curse the people of Israel. The King of Moab knew what we all know: the opinions
of others, especially the opinion of one carrying the authority of a prophet, matters. Their words carry weight. They can
hurt. They can kill.

Many years ago, a man in my parish was diagnosed by a
psychiatrist as bipolar. I do not know how the diagnosis was

made. I only know that the diagnosis was wrong. The young man had just ended a cherished relationship, and he was, quite naturally, devastated. But he was not bipolar. He was not even clinically depressed. But the effect of those words was tremendous. For almost ten years, he waged an internal battle against that false diagnosis. Whenever he had a bad day, his mind would turn to his own self-doubt. Was it true? Was he, in fact, bipolar? If he indeed had been bipolar, then he might have found medication to address his mental state; his life might have improved. But the misdiagnosis only caused him pain. Because he could not find relief in it, the diagnosis haunted him, causing him to doubt everything he did. It was only with enormous courage and good therapy that he emerged ten years later with a new understanding of himself.

I like to gather the youth of our church together around a candle to practice the power of speech. We spend an entire evening doing nothing but building each other up. I have them write down on scraps of paper the gifts and the good that they see in one another. These are the only positive words some of these teens have heard in a long time. One young woman held onto those scraps of paper for years, and when she was feeling her worst, she would pull them out and look at them. Those simple scraps of paper reminded her of her own goodness, of her worth.

To Ponder in Prayer

Waiting for Christ does not just involve watching with our eyes. It also involves speaking with our mouths. We look for glimpses of Christ in one another and then speak those words, identify those gifts. In this way, we edify one another. We begin to believe in the good that others see in us. We begin to believe that Christ might actually want to come back to us in bodily form. We begin to believe that it would be worth his while. Can you edify someone with words today?

Tuesday in Week 3

(To the chief priests and elders) Jesus said, "Truly I tell you, the tax collectors and the prostitutes are going into the kingdom of God ahead of you. For John came to you in the way of righteousness and you did not believe him, but the tax collectors and the prostitutes believed him; and even after you saw it, you did not change your minds and believe him."

—Matthew 21:31b–32

A woman in a parish I once served was drinking herself to death; she consumed at least a gallon of scotch per week. I drove her and her husband to a treatment facility. In that place, we learned a great deal. Alcohol and drug programs must have the consent of the patient who is to be detoxified and treated. To acquire consent, they have a process, a one-two punch, that they take the patient through to make them aware of the severity of the problem.

We sat in a waiting room. First a young woman came in.

Gentle and kind, she led this woman through a series of questions. They began in a benign manner. How old was she? Had she suffered from any medical problems? Then, gradually, the interviewer led her into the realm of alcohol. Did she enjoy drinking? How much did she drink, say, in a day, a week, a month? With each shocking reply, the staff member showed no judgment, but simply recorded the answer and smiled with kindness. When her part was complete, she left, and my friend smiled at me. "This is nothing," she said. "See, I told you there was nothing wrong with my drinking."

Then the doctor arrived. With the papers from the previous session in hand, he pulled his chair right up to my friend, bent down, and looked her directly in the eye. "I am a medical doctor," he explained. "I specialize in the effects of alcohol and toxins on the body. I am here to tell you, in no uncertain terms, that you are killing yourself with alcohol. All of the health problems that you have are alcohol related. If you stop now, you could live a good life, though your liver is permanently damaged. If you continue to drink, you will die."

This doctor spoke in a tone that captivated me. It was anger. It was a warning. It was the naked truth, spoken with a kind of conviction that I will never forget. My friend's husband had come along with us, but the doctor did not even acknowledge his presence. He didn't look at him. The husband's enabling of her drinking appeared to make the doctor think very little of him. Without words, it became clear that the doctor thought that this man ought to be ashamed. His fearful avoidance of confrontation with his wife was as destructive as her alcoholism. And yet, despite the doctor's obvious anger at the wife and his disdain of her husband, I knew, I just knew that this doctor cared about the couple. His anger came from a deep commitment to the treatment of alcoholism.

When Jesus spoke to the chief priests and Pharisees of his day, he spoke in a very similar tone. They thought that they knew about God, but they had become so addicted to traditions and rules that they lost sight of God. They were so busy defending their rules that they missed the greatest event in the history of the world. Jesus was standing right in front of them, the Messiah that they had waited centuries to meet, and they were not able to recognize him. Jesus' anger was born of the same kind of frustration as that doctor in that hospital room. Didn't they see that their blindness was killing them? There are times when it is most appropriate to be angry. Jesus served as a model for the kind of righteous anger that can arise when one is confronted with avoidance, with delusion, with denial.

My friend did not check into the hospital that day, but she did agree to treatment one year later, when her entire family and I confronted her. Remembering the doctor's conviction, I knelt down and looked my friend in the face. She told me that she didn't even care if she died. "You may not be concerned about dying," I said to her, "but I am concerned about the state of your soul." That did it. She got up out of her chair, and we helped her to the car. By this time, she could hardly walk.

To Ponder in Prayer

Jesus' anger at the Pharisees was right, it was necessary, and it was born of love and conviction. Jesus was angry because religious people were worshiping the rules and not God. They had become so addicted to tradition that their minds were closed to revelation. I give thanks for Jesus' anger, his courage. Jesus told it like it was. If a man or woman were full of addiction, he named it. If someone wallowed in self-pity, he named that, too. He did not suffer fools. What will he say to you when he comes again? What will he say when he looks you in the eye?

Wednesday in Week 3

I am the Lord, and there is no other;
besides me there is no god.
I arm you, though you do not know me,
so that they may know, from the rising of the sun
and from the west, that there is no one besides me;
I am the Lord, and there is no other.

—Isaiah 45:5–6

Years ago I worked in an orphanage in the country then known as the Soviet Union. Glasnost and perestroika were close on the horizon. The country was in ruins. Lines of people wrapped around the block. When I asked people what they were waiting for, they often did not know. "We hope that there is some kind of food at the end of the line," they'd say. One day, I waited for three hours in a line for food. When I finally made it into the store, I realized that I could purchase nothing but Cocoa Puffs.

The orphanages were extremely poor. The few toys they had were on display in a cabinet. Though the women who worked there genuinely loved the children, they could not possibly give each child the attention that he or she deserved and needed. The children were lonely and longed to be held. They were starving for affection. I found myself holding them for hours, playing on the playground for hours. Their needs seemed insatiable. At night I would fall into bed exhausted.

Time and time again, the children would ask me to adopt them. But I was still in college. I couldn't. I had to explain that I was there only to be with them for the summer. (Thank heavens that the adoption agency for which I was working would not allow its employees to even consider adoption while working in an orphanage.) And how could I choose just one of them anyway? I loved them all.

In the face of my inability to become a permanent caregiver, I began to tell these children about God. "God is your true Father and your Mother," I would explain. "Though you can't see God, God is with you all of the time, loving you. It is God who will never leave you." The children plied me with questions about this God who was their parent, this God who loved them. "How can we feel him?" they'd ask. "How can we know him?" I would take them to the Russian Orthodox church in their village. "Come here," I'd say. "Here is a special place where it is often easier to hear and feel God."

I could see the seeds of faith planted in the hearts of

these children. They had something to hope for, someone to long for. They asked me numerous questions about God: Did God really love them? Was God with them all the time? Could they talk to God? I could see a new light of hope in their eyes. How many of them would learn to trust that hope? How many would find that God was there just as I had promised? I will never know. The path of these children's lives was to grow harder as they grew older. The home for teens, to which they would "graduate," was rife with crime and drugs. Would they be able to hold onto that faith, that hope in God? Would they come to church?

The hope that Isaiah gave the people of Israel was not so different from the hope that I tried to give those children. How is it that some of us choose to believe while others cannot? I saw how hope alone gave those children something to hold onto. If they could just cling to that hope, they just might weather the storm of their own hard lives.

To Ponder in Prayer

The existence of God that Isaiah confirms can serve as a source of strength, of grounding for people. If there is a God, then someone cares what I do. Someone cares that children are hungry. Someone longs for people to tell the truth and knows when we tell a lie. Someone sees when we steal and we think that no one is looking. When Isaiah declares these words, "I am God and there is no other," he is affirming right and wrong, the meaning of life itself. We would be lost without that promise. The hope of God's presence, the hope of God's coming. It is a powerful thing. It can sustain lives.

Thursday in Week 3

Do not fear, for you will not be ashamed....
—Isaiah 54:4

"Stress?" said one of the women in a parish I served. "Oh, I don't really have to deal with stress or anxiety," she explained. Funny, I thought, because she seemed totally dominated by fear. She seemed compelled to keep order in everything that she did. Mistakes were simply not tolerated. I feared for her small son, who was not free to play in the mud, not free to get a bad grade. By the age of five, he had developed a nervous twitch.

One of the greatest obstacles to the growth of a church is fear. Fear of the unknown, of the unexpected. When a new minister arrives in a parish, one of the most commonly asked questions is: "Are you going to change anything?" They may have even hired a new minister to grow the church, to lead them into the future. But often they are so afraid that they are unwilling to move. At least not too quickly, not too far. So the minister is constantly fighting a battle with an unseen and unnamed fear. How far will the parish be willing to go in Christ's footsteps before the fear takes over and halts any movement forward?

Today, fear often manifests around issues of money. If people are afraid, they will not pledge. If they do not give, we cannot move forward in building, in doing ministry. "We want change," we may say, "but we can't afford it." What is lack of money? Is it simply the congregation saying that the ministry we are considering is either too scary or just not important enough to merit their money?

We are right to be afraid. Jesus teaches that the truly Christian life is nothing if not scary. It is a constant journey in the footsteps of one who died on a cross. It is a life of obedience to God and to no other—not money, not family, not career, nothing. No wonder we are afraid.

When you boil down life to its essential nature, we are simply tiny creatures living in a huge universe, and we do not know, we cannot know, what the future will hold. Because we can conceive of the future but not predict it, we are constantly afraid. No matter how much we schedule our days ahead and stick to routines, the element of novelty and change is always present. No one day looks like another. Everything is constantly changing around us.

Years ago, I took a workshop on faith. One of the participants drew a picture of what faith meant to him. In the picture, there was a man standing on the edge of a cliff. He was about to step out into the abyss beyond the cliff. It looked as if he might fall, but he had faith that something, somewhere would hold him up. He had a look of sheer determination on his face. He seemed determined to be alive.

Every person dies, but who really lives? Only those who are willing to move beyond fear. I have written for years to a woman who lives in a tiny apartment alone. She wants to leave her job, which makes her miserable, but she is afraid. So she stays, and year after year, I get a card from her. "How are you?" she writes, "I am still here." If she could conquer her fear, her life would be larger. But fear keeps her imprisoned in a small, small world.

To Ponder in Prayer
Do not be afraid, the prophet says. Take that step. Don't ever choose to resist life simply because of fear. Whenever we risk living, we anticipate the coming of Christ. We act on the belief that Christ will return and we will be all right. Is your fear preventing you from living the life that you want to live?

Friday in Week 3

Thus says the Lord God,
who gathers the outcasts of Israel,
I will gather others to them
besides those already gathered.

—Isaiah 56:8

If the Church ever really learned how to market community, we'd be busting at the seams. If we could ever articulate the wholeness that comes from knowing that there is a group of people who accept you, who know your limitations and your faults, and love you anyway; if we could express what it feels like to be accepted, to be included into a body of people; if we could ever learn to spell this out, we'd be in business. But community—the void that it can fill, the contentment that it can bring—is inexpressible. And that is why you never can sell church. It cannot be accurately or adequately conveyed to an outsider. Church, community, must be experienced to be understood.

Of course, every congregation is different. Some are not communities so much as cliques, destructive groups of people who thrive on the exclusion of some, the rejection of some. But many churches, despite feuds over the altar flowers, despite members who carry a twenty-year-old grudge because the minister didn't visit them in the hospital, still catch glimpses of community.

The church where I am now serving recently celebrated Mardi Gras after a long hiatus. Years ago, the annual Mardi Gras celebration was popular, but it had fallen by the wayside and had not been celebrated for some time. This year, the party was a hit. There was laughter, there was food, there was fun. The choir sang an outrageous medley of Broadway tunes matched with lyrics written about all the characters of the parish. We sang about our love of the church. We danced. The preschoolers danced a jig with the grandmothers while a child-prodigy sax player wowed us all with his funky jazz. For a moment there, as I looked out over the dance floor, I knew I'd caught a glimpse of the Kingdom of God.

Isaiah speaks of such a gathering at the coming of the Messiah. There will be a reconciliation. People will be gathered together in one place. Even the outcasts will be brought into the fold. There will be no more exclusion, only community. When Christ draws all of us to the Divine self, we will be drawn to one another.

What will this Kingdom of God look like? I'm not entirely sure, but I believe that we know its opposite. We know the horrors of war, oppression, division. But the Kingdom itself? That can only come to us in scattered moments, in tastes of reconciliation that leave us hungry for more. We spend our lives searching for this kind of unity and understanding.

When my husband and I were first married, we left the reception in a jeep covered with streamers and Just Married regalia. We were scheduled to fly out of Kennedy International Airport on our honeymoon the next day. On the morning after the wedding, we found ourselves driving into New York City in our decorated jeep. I have always hated the interstate highway that leads to New York City. It is crowded and dirty, and people are rude. But not on that morning. No, there must have been something about our Just Married sign that crossed all cultural boundaries. Old cars, chock full of guys on their way to work, pulled over to let us in while they honked and cheered. Little elderly ladies in Cadillacs waved. Even a juiced-up black BMW moved aside to let us into a line at the tollbooth. That morning, I caught a glimpse of the Kingdom, that place where people of all races, colors, and creeds celebrate love itself together. For a moment there, on a highway at rush hour, I knew that such a thing was possible, and it made me smile.

To Ponder in Prayer

The Kingdom of God cannot be described, it cannot be programmed, but it can be glimpsed. We are waiting for a kind of community that each one of us has tasted or seen in moments, in priceless moments. You will recognize God's kingdom if you find yourself, from time to time, catching intimacy's shadow, seeing beauty that is present one moment and gone the next. Catch these glimpses, and know that there is so much more to come.

December 17–24

December 17

In his days may righteousness flourish
and peace abound, until the moon is no more.

—Psalm 72:7

I've resisted watching the news and reading newspapers for most of my life. I used to think I was "too busy." Looking back, I know that was just an excuse. My first bishop had told me clearly that as an Episcopal priest, I would need three things at hand at all times: a Bible, a Book of Common Prayer, and a newspaper. But my resistance to the news ran deeper than being just a matter of busyness. I was overwhelmed by the state of the world.

Day after day, night after night, we hear of pain and struggle. Countries torn apart by civil discord. Rulers depriving people of the simple blessing of freedom. Innocent people who are imprisoned, murdered. It seems that good news is simply not as interesting to the general population.

We are not all that interested in the young man who works in the inner-city teaching kids. Instead we want to hear about the man who raped and killed twelve women before he was finally arrested. The media both feeds on tragedy and serves us a banquet of it every day.

When I was younger, I found myself simply incapable of absorbing so much violence and pain. So I changed the channel or neglected to renew my subscription to the paper. But you cannot comfort people if you do not understand their predicament. I was not as good a priest as I might have been because I avoided the world scene. Gradually, as I grew older, I tried to change my ways. Today I believe that one of the most important aspects of my ministry is listening to my city and to the world. Where is the pain? How might the Scripture give us insight into our struggles? What is God saying *now?*

Maybe one of the reasons bad news sells so well is that it still surprises us. Human beings, no matter how war-worn or battle-scarred, seem to expect goodness. Tragedy still surprises us. We cannot believe that it's happening. When a little girl disappears without a trace from our community, we find it hard to believe, hard to accept. Who would do such a thing? Can it really be possible?

The very expectation of goodness is what leads me to believe in the Kingdom of God. We would not be so disappointed when our lives are hard were it not for the fact that we were created for Eden. People constantly come up to me in church asking what they have done to deserve such difficulties. "Why is God punishing me?" they ask. "What did I do to deserve this?" Recently a woman, balding from the effects of chemotherapy, approached me after an adult education session and asked, "Why does God do this to us?"

Why are we so surprised by suffering? Why does it seem so wrong? Because God did not create us to exist in such a world. No, we did that ourselves when we ate the fruit that God forbade us to eat. It is crucial that we clarify the fact that we caused this fall. God did not do it. We did it. God did not will our suffering. No, our suffering is caused by the consequences of our free will. We chose to disobey. We chose to live our lives our way. And nothing has seemed right since. Suffering seems so wrong because it *is* wrong. It is not what God originally intended.

That is why the coming of Christ is so right. The pieces of our world that don't fit together, the pain that is rampant around us—all that will be made right. There will be peace; peace that none of us can understand, but that all of us somehow anticipate.

When I worked in an orphanage in Russia, the children all hoped and dreamed about having a mother and a father. They couldn't stop hoping, talking about it, asking why they did not have anyone. Why did they do this? Because even at such a young age, they knew that their situation was aberrant. It was not right. They should have had parents. They deserved parents. They knew, deep down inside, that things should not be as they were. They knew that they belonged in families. The dream of Eden could not be taken from them.

To Ponder in Prayer

The dream of Christ's world cannot be taken away from us. It is where we belong. It is what we were made for. The world doesn't feel right to us because it isn't home. For now, we must live between two worlds—the one we know and the one that is still to come. When Christ comes, we will come Home.

December 18

He has pity on the weak and the needy,
and saves the lives of the needy.

—Psalm 72:13

About five years ago, my husband gave up the practice of law to direct a soup kitchen. The soup kitchen, which was located in the back of a large, downtown Presbyterian church, fed up to four hundred people each day, and whenever I could, I would go down and help. I was always surprised by the clientele. These were not just men and women living on the street. There were entire families coming in: women with tiny babies, families with five children and both parents. Many were the working poor. Their jobs paid such low wages that they could afford rent or food, but not both. They chose to pay their rent and come to the soup kitchen for food.

"How did I end up so well-off?" I would wonder to myself as I spooned another pile of beans onto a plate. Was being born kind of like the lottery? Was I just lucky? What makes me so different from the people eating here? Nothing but a few paychecks and maybe a few academic degrees.

My son Luke is consumed with fairness these days. If his younger brother, Jacob, holds onto the toy longer than he had it, I will hear the same phrase over and over again. Luke shouts it at the top of his lungs: *"It's not fair!"* And he's right. It isn't fair. Life isn't fair.

Fairness is just not woven into the fabric of the world. Why are some children abused and others loved? Why do illnesses occur in some young people and not in others? We can explain the "how" of these questions (because the parents hit the child or because the cells in a certain person's body grew cancerous) but we simply cannot address the "why." So we all join my four-year-old with our own *"It's not fair!"* When we tire of screaming it, we internalize it, but the cry remains.

Almost every day, someone comes to me with what I now call a "why question." Why do bad things happen to good people? Why is the world unfair? Why did such a terrible thing happen to me? I can never answer. I dole out all of the theological musings that I have collected over my lifetime. I hand these to people in the hopes that these thoughts give them some comfort, but the question remains.

I do not believe that God purposefully causes suffering. Suffering is a result of our free will. With the choice to love comes the choice to run away from God, to hurt others and all of the suffering that goes along with that. We live in a world that we helped to shape when we disobeyed God in Eden. We live in a world where we affect our own destiny. It is called freedom. Yes, God can intervene, and God will help us if asked, but mostly God leaves us free to return in love. And sometimes still, bad things happen to good people.

Though we can never fully comprehend the "why question," I do believe that we must do something about the state of the world. I have always believed that we cannot simply wait passively for the coming of Christ. We must try to create Christ's justice on earth even before the Second Coming. Whenever we hand a bowl of soup to someone who is hungry, we bring the reality of Christ's coming just a bit closer. We can affect the world through our hope, our efforts, our actions. While living in an unfair world, we can act as if things were fair. We can treat others with respect, no matter where they may be in life. We can *make* the Kingdom of God a reality, one step at a time.

I find that there is nothing that feeds my soul quite like helping another person. If I can help someone when I am feeling low, often my heart will start to warm, my anger will begin to melt. The best kind of therapy is anticipating God's Kingdom.

To Ponder in Prayer

With each decision to help another person, we become closer
to the One for whom we wait. You can catch glimpses of the
Kingdom in the eyes of the man who has heard a kind word
and filled his belly. When he looks at you and asks for a second helping, you wonder if you might have just caught a
glimpse of your Lord. What can you do today to bring a bit of
justice to the world?

December 19

*And the angel of the Lord appeared to the woman and said to
her, "Although you are barren, having borne no children, you
shall conceive and bear a son.... It is he who shall begin to
deliver Israel from the hand of the Philistines."*

—Judges 13: 3, 5b

*But the angel said to him, "Do not be afraid, Zechariah, for
your prayer has been heard. Your wife Elizabeth will bear
you a son, and you will name him John.... He will turn
many of the people of Israel to the Lord their God."*

—Luke 1:13, 16

Samson and John both had rough lives. Samson was strong
and battled the Philistines, but he ended up blind and in
chains on the day of his reckoning. Yes, he took many
Philistines down with him when he pulled their temple down
on his own head, but he died a gruesome death. John also led

a harsh life. He spent his time in the heat of the desert. He ate bugs and honey and dressed in camel's hair. Eventually, he was arrested and beheaded by the king. Both Samson and John lived irregular lives and died violently.

And these were servants of God. The Bible sure does not sugarcoat its stories. This is no recruitment spiel. God does not try to sell us on service. The Scripture is brutally truthful about the fact that those who served God often were lonely, outcast, misunderstood, and even killed.

Yet, time and time again, we expect a reward for our devotion. We believe that following the will of God means getting something good for our efforts. Success, popularity, acclaim: those are the things that ought to find us if we follow God's will. The message is all over the church. Look at this pastor, he or she doubled their church attendance in two years. God is in that place! The media adds to the hype by profiling success. The more effective the evangelism, the closer it must be to the service of Christ. We must learn how to advertise correctly, market our message, and God will be with us.

According to Scripture, however, the true servants of God are often hated. They can be left alone to die as outcasts. They are the man on the street corner, the one who slept under a bridge last night. The one who used to own a small business, but tried to tell the truth about his colleagues and got in trouble. The one who refused to destroy documents in the law firm and got fired. The one who started drinking a lot to forget the price that he paid for his honesty. Those are the prophets. Those are their rewards.

How can we measure our faithfulness? Maybe the very concept of measuring it is not godly. The Bible never seems to care about exact figures, about numbers. The measuring stick of the One who is to come is very different from our own. Success is not the issue, nor is popularity, nor is the number of billable hours. Truth is the issue. Truth and courage and love—above all else the love of God.

To Ponder in Prayer
Would you be willing to die for God? When the rest of the world hated you, would you trust that you were loved? Perhaps the best sign of devotion is the willingness to give all of this life up for God. Can we stand up and oppose injustice in the face of everyone that we love? That was ultimately what John and Samson did. It is a scary journey, this Christian one. It seems that the closer we get to Christ, the more we must leave behind.

December 20

The angel said to [Mary], "The Holy Spirit will come upon you, and the power of the Most High will overshadow you; therefore the child to be born will be holy; he will be called Son of God."... Then Mary said, "Here am I, the servant of the Lord; let it be with me according to your word."

—Luke 1:35, 38

I once heard an old piece of folklore about Mary. Imagine, this story goes, that the angel of God had been wandering the earth since the beginning of time, asking people if they would be willing to bring God's child into the world. Mary was not the most pure, most holy, most beautiful; she was simply the only one gutsy enough to say "yes."

I love that little addition to the Gospel narrative because it makes us look at the story from a different angle. The Church has traditionally taught us that Mary was selected by God for the most important task of all time, the birth of Christ.

Mary is seen as the most pure, the most devout woman in the
world. She was selected, out of all the women of all time, to be
the mother of God. It's almost as if Mary is the valedictorian
of devotion, she was the best, and she was awarded the greatest
honor. But what if her role was awarded to her because she
alone was willing, because she agreed? What if it was Mary's
willingness that set her apart?

In the Gospel of Luke, Mary says to the angel Gabriel,
"Here am I." These are words repeated by some of the most
devout lovers of God in Scripture. Abraham says, "Here I
am." Isaiah says "Here I am." These are the words of those
who volunteer to submit themselves to the will of God. These
are the words of true devotion. After uttering these words, no
one ever stands still.

But most of the time, I don't say "Here I am." Instead, I
think that my prayer, subconsciously, may be along the lines
of "Here I am, but don't disturb me too much, God." Why do
I say this? Because it is so scary to simply say "Here I am."
That kind of willingness can throw your whole life into a tizzy.
That kind of devotion takes courage that I don't have. I want
to follow God's will when it's comfortable to do so. If God
asks too much, I pretend to be deaf. I stop listening. I think,
maybe I need a vacation. Most of us don't say "yes" to God;
we say, "Yes, but…."

A woman once called and asked to see me immediately. She was having marital problems and didn't know

what to do. I met her late one night at the church, and she unfolded her story.

"I feel trapped in my marriage," she said. "I am a sinner. My good Catholic parents tell me to stick it out, but my soul feels like it is shrinking. I feel so trapped at home that my chest feels tight as I drive closer to the house. Why do I feel this way? I cannot even go to church. Help me." She was convinced that she was a terrible sinner and could not understand why her heart kept telling her to leave her husband.

At a loss, I asked her more about her life with her husband. Slowly, she began to describe his behavior. She told of a raging alcoholic, a man who was drinking himself to death. Refusing to accept that there was anything wrong with his behavior, he accused her of being ugly, too critical and restless. Meanwhile he was drinking gallons of bourbon every few days. He would wake up multiple times at night to drink more, go to the bathroom, and then fall back into a dead stupor. Lately, he had taken to grabbing her and hitting her son.

"I know that I am supposed to be obedient," she said, "But I feel like I am dying."

I began to explain the disease of alcoholism. We talked about treatment possibilities, about her husband's violence. Slowly, I tried to explain that God actually might not want her to watch her husband drink himself to death. We talked about the fact that she must make it clear that he is not to drink, or he will have to leave their house. We talked about the fact that he could turn violent and rage. She might have to get a restraining order. We talked about how difficult it might be to get him into treatment.

"How could God be asking me to do this?" she cried. "This is just so hard. It's so active. I don't know if I have the strength." Gradually, she came to the conclusion that love would have her battle her husband's alcoholism. But in doing so, she must agree to a world of conflict and pain.

It can be so hard to say "yes" to God. Most of us just think that we haven't heard right. "You can't want me to do that, we say, but that's too hard, too painful. That won't make me look good, that would be messy, crazy, and frightening. "Yes," we say to God, "yes, but later, but not this way, but maybe I'll just wait for another day." It's easier to say "maybe later" than it is to say "yes" to love in all its potency.

To Ponder in Prayer

"Here I am, Lord." These words will mean so many different things for different people. But for all of us, they mean that we must make room for active, true love in our lives. We must follow the truth even if it costs us pain, estrangement, and judgment from others. Listen deep into your heart for these words. Where will they lead you?

December 21

*When Elizabeth heard Mary's greeting, the child leaped in
her womb. And Elizabeth was filled with the Holy Spirit and
exclaimed with a loud cry, "Blessed are you among women,
and blessed is the fruit of your womb."* —Luke 1:41–42

An unspoken connection exists among pregnant women,
a silent knowing. When I was pregnant with my sons, and now
in the years that have followed, I gravitate toward pregnant
women. I want to know how they feel. Can they feel the baby
moving? Are they comfortable, hot, do their feet ache? The
gravitation toward other women who are having babies is
strong and primal. We understand the mysterious joy of feeling life inside of our own bodies. We know what it's like. Together, we learn from one another.

When I was pregnant with my first child, I formed a
mothers' group. We met once a month for about two hours.
Older women from the church volunteered to watch our ba-

bies in the nursery while we talked. We became quite intimate, crying and laughing together. It was great to express feelings that no one else seemed to understand—that pang of hunger for chocolate cake at two A.M.; the need to weep for no reason at all; the sheer exhaustion of trying to nurse a newborn. We taught one another. Together, we realized how blessed we were to be part of this incredible cosmic dance called birth. The group helped me know myself as a woman. They helped me see that I was a good mother. They laughed at my insecurities. Together, we prayed for our children. It was the kind of spontaneous community that one finds only occasionally in life, the kind that can make you feel part of something much greater than yourself.

I imagine that Elizabeth and Mary formed this kind of bond. They found themselves physically moved to be in each other's presence. They must have been lonely and frightened—an old woman and a young woman, unwed at that. They must have found strength in each other, in their companionship.

It says in the Scripture that the child in Elizabeth's womb leaped. This makes sense to me because Elizabeth was further along in her pregnancy than Mary. Her child was more fully developed and would have had the capacity to jump in the belly. This happens frequently, and it can be quite jolting. I used to call my son Luke "Jumping Bean" when he was inside my belly. When he leaped, it could make me jump, too.

It means a great deal to me that the mother of God needed companionship when she was pregnant with the Christ. Mary needed a friend to help her understand her pregnancy. She needed the support of friendship. It sustained her.

We, too, need the support and sustenance of friendships. We must nurture those relationships that are naturally supportive. Mary and Elizabeth used their friendship to understand God's work in and through them. We, too, can utilize those relationships that bring us a clearer understanding of our own selves, our vocations, our lives.

Would Mary and Elizabeth have realized how truly blessed they were if they had not seen each other? I don't think that they would have known the full extent of the gift that God had given each of them. It often takes another person to help us see ourselves more clearly. We cannot know ourselves completely without the feedback of another.

To Ponder in Prayer

Late one night, my son Luke could not sleep. "I having bad dreams," he said through his tears. "Well, Jesus is here with you," I said, hoping that my answer would suffice and he could go back to sleep. "But I want Jesus with skin on," he said. Sometimes we need the touch and love of a living person, and that relationship helps us to wait for Christ to come. How are you nurturing the important relationships in your life?

December 22

*And [Hannah] said, "Oh, my lord! As you live, my lord, I am
the woman who was standing here in your presence, praying
to the Lord. For this child I prayed; and the Lord has granted
me the petition that I made to him. Therefore I have lent him
to the Lord; as long as he lives, he is given to the Lord."*

—I Samuel 26–27

She gave up her *child.* I have a hard time giving up one
hour's sleep. I struggle to give up just a small portion of my
money. Forget my child. I am not even close to that! I am not
even close to giving that kind of a gift back to God. I would
have said "thank you" for my son. "Oh, thank you so much."
But if God had asked anything more of me, well, I probably
would have pretended that I hadn't heard right. God couldn't *possibly* want me to bring my child to some old man to be
raised away from me. No, I must have heard wrong.

How many of your deepest prayers have been answered? Have you ever considered how much of what you have really belongs to God? Is it not everything? So how can we begin to repay the Creator? These thoughts seem overwhelming to most of us, because we have been raised in a culture that focuses not on giving, but on consuming. The world of capitalism feeds on our own insatiable hunger to gratify ourselves. Just a few weeks ago, I visited a mall. It was gorgeous—four stories tall, with a glass-domed ceiling. When you walk inside, you are greeted with fountains, statues, plants, and flowers. A piano magically plays show tunes by itself. "This is a temple," I thought to myself, "this is a temple to the god of materialism. If aliens were to land here in the United States, they would surely think that this place is where we worship."

Feed yourself, the media says, and you will be happy. Buy something more for yourself, you deserve it. Clothe yourself in the best, even if you have to take it out on loan. Everything ought to belong to you. If you only had more, you would be happy. If you only owned it all, you would be gloriously happy!

And we buy it. We go to the clothing department and see the most beautiful jacket we have ever seen. We think, "That's it! If I could just wear that, I'd look like a million bucks!" We buy the jacket, though it costs too much (and we know it). We take it home. The next morning, we look at the jacket, hanging in our overstuffed closet, and it just looks like . . . a jacket. The magic is gone, and we are left with more credit card debt. What happened?

We are far away from the generosity of Hannah. We have been lured by the empty promises of the god of the mall. We believe that focusing on our own well-being will make us happy. We feel a sense of privilege, that we deserve the best, and if the best doesn't come our way, well, something is wrong.

Hannah had waited for years to have a child. She had been barren. Her barreness must have hurt her, each and every day. She went to the temple to pray for a son. Bearing a male child was the sole means of gaining respect for a woman of her time. And when Samuel came, she knew that he had never been hers to begin with.

No wonder the poor are blessed by God. If you are poor, you know whatever comes to you comes as a gift from God. As one who is poor, you know that you have nothing, and so everything is worthy of thanks and praise. You are aware of what God does for you, every moment of every day.

More than perhaps anything else, our wealth and privilege prevent us from understanding the generosity of God. Our supposed ownership of things prevents us from experiencing the emptiness that only God can fill. Sure, we still have that emptiness, but as long as we fill it with new things, with food, with alcohol, or with money, we will not be leaving room for Christ to come and fill the void with the presence of God.

To Ponder in Prayer

Hannah generously gave her child back to God, and by so doing, a prophet came to be. Mary generously gave herself, and Jesus Christ came to be. What would happen if, from this point on, we generously gave our lives to God? Would the Christ then have a place to return? How might generosity pave the way for the return of Christ?

December 23

But who can endure the day of his coming,
and who can stand when he appears?

— Malachi 3:2

Almost seven years ago, I thought I heard God's voice. My husband, J. D., and I were in Israel, visiting the Holy Land for the first time. We decided not to sign up with a tour, but to go on our own, with two large backpacks and a lot of sunblock. The trip changed my understanding of the Scripture, and it changed my relationship with God.

Toward the end of our time in Israel, we returned to Jerusalem to visit the Church of the Holy Sepulchre, the church that stands over Golgotha and the tomb of Christ.

We entered the church at five A.M. We knelt at the place where Jesus was crucified, we felt the rock that must have been there at the hill called "the Skull." It was burnished smooth by the caress of the hands of millions of pilgrims. My mind was beyond thought; I was simply experiencing something that I knew would impact my entire life.

At last, we entered the tomb where Jesus was raised from the dead. There are two chambers in the tomb. We knelt inside the outer cave and listened as a Catholic priest said the mass in Spanish. As we knelt on the stone floor, he came to us and put a wafer in our mouths. He did not ask us where we were from, what denomination we were. We simply opened our mouths and received communion. Such a feeding of my soul was—and is—beyond words.

The next day, J. D. wanted to return to the church, but I didn't want to go. I didn't want to go back when our communion in the tomb had been so perfect, so complete. I didn't want to have any other memory of the place. And besides, it was the middle of the afternoon. It couldn't possible be as holy as it was, and I didn't want to remember it any other way.

But J. D. insisted. I could see that it really mattered to him, so I consented. I tagged along, though I believed that I had experienced Christ's presence once and that was all I could ask.

We entered the church, and, unlike the morning before, there were hundreds of people milling about. The Orthodox, Coptics, and Catholics have divided up the church into sections, and they quarrel with one another about which holy spot belongs to which denomination. The Coptics were chanting upstairs, the Orthodox were fussing over some candles, and there was a long line in front of the entrance to the tomb.

I just knelt at a rail near the tomb. I closed my eyes. In a moment of simplicity that is rare for me, I told God that I was simply content to be where I was. I thanked God. Then I heard, "Come inside." Just two words. "Come inside."

How can I explain? The voice was not my own, and yet it was like the very best of me and more. It was the healthiest, strongest voice that I have ever heard. It has taken me seven years just to write about it, but not a day goes by when I don't think about that voice. It was the most wonderful, most terrifying thing that has ever happened to me in my life. I hear echoes of that voice in the very best of myself, and I hear its absence in every misjudgment I make.

Come inside. Those were the words. I looked up. The line in front of the tomb was gone. I walked inside because I had been told to do so. I went into the inner tomb. There was a basket for offerings, so I emptied my pockets, feeling secretly relieved that I did not bring my entire savings with me. Then a security guard came in. "How did you get in here alone?" he demanded. "Where is the money? You haven't taken the money, have you?" I didn't say anything, as he emptied the basket into another bag. I walked out of the tomb and into the next chapter of my life.

The part that puzzles me the most is how afraid I am of hearing that voice again—how afraid I am of looking at the one who spoke, and yet how much I long for that encounter as well. That voice was so good, so very whole and well that I almost couldn't stand it. Those two words have echoed through my life since. How could I withstand more? I know that when I hear that voice again, I will do whatever it asks of me. I am afraid of what I will be asked.

To Ponder in Prayer

Have you ever tried to look at the sun? We cannot do it. It blinds us. So we will not be able to stand when Christ appears. We will fall on our faces and beg forgiveness, full of fear and joy. Are you afraid to hear the voice of God? What is it that God might ask of you? How will you respond?

December 24

By the tender mercy of our God,
the dawn from on high will break upon us,
to give light to those who sit in darkness and in the shadow of death,
to guide our feet into the way of peace. —Luke 1:78–79

I like to read books over and over again. If I've had a hard day, I will fix a plate of comfort food—pickles and raisins and stuff that I ate as a child—and I lie down on the sofa with a book that I have read many times before. I love to savor the words and not have to worry about the outcome. I know the end of the story. I know who will win the battle, so I can sit back and enjoy.

You might say that not knowing the "ending" of our stories causes us to be fearful, that it casts shadows on our lives. The present is more or less clear. In the present moment, we can see and hear and determine our actions within certain parameters. The past we can see, though it is a bit grayer, especially as we grow further away from it. But the future is simply darkness. We cannot see it, we cannot determine it. It is beyond our control and, therefore, terrifying. We are creatures crawling forward in darkness. No wonder we crave routine and order. No wonder child psychologists tell us to establish a daily schedule for a toddler and follow it closely. At least we give, in this small way, the illusion of security. It's no wonder that I like to read books over and over again; at least I know what is going to happen. But ministry in the church changes every day.

Zechariah was right—we sit in darkness. We cannot see ahead; we see behind us only for a short while. The greatest unknown for us is death. We sit in the shadow of death. It looms over us. All of us will die; the only question is when. That ultimate reality, the *only* unchangeable factor in our lives, hangs over us like a shadow, and we run from it as fast as we can. We may try to pretend that it isn't there, but it does not go away.

A certain amount of fear, a healthy respect for the future—these are signs of sanity. We rightly respect the future if we are looking with clear vision at the state of our lives. The future is unknown. Anyone who pretends that they can control their destiny is laboring under a delusion. We are in the shadow of death.

No wonder we war with one another. Our lives are filled with fear. Perhaps if the other country gets a nuclear weapon, we might die sooner rather than later. At least we can prevent them from acquiring one, and maybe that will push back the shadow just a bit. No wonder we fight. Fear and anger are so intertwined. We fear oblivion. We fear being alone.

When the dawn from on high breaks upon us, it will illumine everything more clearly. We will be given the capacity to see the workings of the universe with great clarity, to witness them even if we can't understand them. Christ will make many things clear for us that have not been clear. We may even be able to see the past and the future as God does. We may be able to return to the people that we have loved. We may be able to see our great-great grandchildren.

To Ponder in Prayer

Zechariah prophesied in the language of poetry. No wonder. How else could he anticipate the coming of God to humans? How can we talk about it in any other way but in the language of art and images? How could there be any other way?

Think of the sunrise and imagine God's clarity entering into your consciousness, enabling you to see more than you have ever seen before. Imagine the breadth and scope of God's vision. Can you catch a glimpse of such wisdom, of such beauty?

Christmas

I once saw a black-and-white photograph of a Palestinian boy, alone in the ruins of a bombed-out building in the West Bank. Dust, dirt, and rubble surrounded him on every side as he stood beneath a blue sky. There he stood, in the midst of destruction, playing music on some kind of wind instrument. It looked like a recorder, but it had been made from the barrel of a gun. He stood amidst the worst horrors of life, and he made music. When I looked at the picture, I wondered how that music might have sounded.

The world in which we live is as violent and crazy as it has ever been. The social and political fabric of the Middle East is in shreds. The Holy Land of Israel is the scene of mass murder. Women are captured in Eastern Europe and sold as slaves in Bosnia. In our town, three teenagers were killed just two days ago. They had been drinking and had run, head on, into a telephone poll. It would be easy to be hopeless.

Not long ago, a young college student sat in my office. His mother was dying of cancer. The chemotherapy that her doctors prescribed had made her go blind. She was bald and blind, and yet she still held onto the hope that she might get better. It was harder for her son.

"Why do I even bother staying alive?" this young man asked. "Why bother to behave myself, to respect the rights of people, to tell the truth? Why treat the earth with care or feed the hungry? Why should I bother with all of that crap when the world is so unfair! My mother is dying and I can't do a damned thing about it!"

Why should we play music in the midst of this mess?

God became a human being today. That means that God descended into *this* world, our world. Jesus was not born into some fairy tale, some peaceful starry night where there was no pain or sorrow or suffering. This holy night was not holy because it was otherworldly or idyllic, it was holy because he was here. He came *here*, into the mess that is our world.

Jesus was born in a cave where the animals slept. It was dirty and smelly. He was born in a country that was ruled by a man so violent and volatile that he would kill babies to appease his paranoia. Jesus was born under a government that thought nothing of forcing a pregnant woman to travel for hundreds of miles to be counted in a census. His mother was a number and nothing more. Jesus was born into a world very much like the one in which we live in today. Jesus came—he came to play music in the midst of this mess.

My mother-in-law has lived in Memphis most of her life. She tells me people come from all over the country to see Graceland, the place where Elvis Presley lived. It is almost as if there were a piece of Elvis somewhere there; it is hallowed ground for thousands. They come just to sit there and look, hoping to catch something of his spirit.

In an odd way, Christians treat one another with kindness not because the world is a great place, but because God was here. God was here, and somehow God's presence is anticipated in everything that we see, in everything that we do. Why treat the planet with care? Because Christ walked on it. Why be good to one another? Because the next person you see could be him. We look for him everywhere because he was here, and he told us he was coming again. Maybe that is why we continue to play music in the midst of this mess.

There is a wonderful scene in the movie *Ordinary People*. The teenaged boy, who has witnessed the death of his older brother in a boating accident, has reached a critical moment in his therapy. All of the pain and fear of the night that his brother died have returned for him. He calls his psychiatrist in the middle of the night from a payphone on the street, having raced out of his house in panic. The therapist meets him at his office. Once in the office, the boy breaks down and cries. He sobs in fear, paces frantically, and then looks at the doctor in anguish. "I'm afraid," he says, "I'm so afraid." And the doctor says the most simple thing. He says, "I'm here. I'm your friend. You can count on it."

I'm here.

That is what the Incarnation of God is about. God is

here. God is with us. "I am here," says the Holy One. "I know that you are in pain, suffering. I am here with you. I have not abandoned you. I am here."

To Ponder in Prayer

There is no greater comfort than the presence of someone who loves you. No words could explain God's love to us. No prophesies or visions had been able to convince us of that presence. So God came. Just to be here with us.

Conclusion

Last night I stepped into the room of a woman who was dying. Her family had gathered for last rites, not knowing exactly when she would breathe her last. The atmosphere in that room was electric. It always is when someone is dying and the family has to say good-bye. We recited those beautiful, ancient words from the Book of Common Prayer. It was about nine o'clock at night. Then I gave the family a chance to say their good-byes.

This woman will no longer be with her family bodily. But somehow, she will remain with them. This new kind of spiritual presence is a mystery to me, but I cannot deny its reality. People come to me all the time saying that they feel the influence of their loved one who died.

This is the best analogy that I can make to the presence of God. In Advent, we wait for Christ to come. Much of the Christian life is spent waiting for the Second Coming. And yet, at the same time, God is with us here. In some mysterious way, God has always been here and will continue to be with us.

When I say my prayers now, I no longer ask for God to be present. I take that presence for granted. Jesus promised us that his Advocate would remain with us, and I believe his words. The more I count on that presence, the more that I feel it anchoring my entire life.

Perhaps the greatest theologians of our day are quantum physicists. As they uncover new dimensions in time and space, the mysteries of the Divine seem more possible, more real. It may be that God indeed exists in a dimension that is far beyond our understanding. It may be that God is with us on levels far beyond our understanding.

But we still want to see Jesus. We want to touch him, to see him smile. And that is why we wait. We wait to experience Christ with us physically, as Jesus once was. I find that the more I acknowledge my hunger for Christ's bodily presence with me, the more I realize my love for God. We miss Christ just as that family will miss their mother, with pangs of grief and longing.

The reunion between Christ and his Church will be one to behold. I myself can't wait to see it.

Acknowledgements

The writing of this book sprang naturally out of my work as a priest. It has been a wonderful discipline for me to write these meditations, and I wish to thank Cowley Publications for the opportunity to do so.

I wish to acknowledge the many people who have contributed to my ministry as an Episcopal priest. Even as a young child, I felt the presence of true community in church. It is this church community that has sustained me and upheld me all these years. Though the particular churches changed, the body of Christ has always functioned in the same way for me, and I am eternally grateful.

My thanks go out to Trinity Church-on-the-Green, the church that baptized me and nurtured me as a child, the Rev. Andrew Fiddler, and the Rev. Ellen Tillotson. To my many mentors along the way: the Rev. Brad Rundlett, the Rev. Bernie Dooley, the Rev. Dena Bearl, the Rev. Gus Weltsek, the

Very Rev. Martha Horne, the Rev. Richard Downing, the Rev. Joe Pace, the Rev. Elizabeth Orens, the Rev. Susan Sharpe, and the Rev. Dennis Smith. To the parishes and the beloved people with whom I have served: St. John's Cathedral in Jacksonville, Florida; St. Timothy's Church in Herndon, Virginia; St. James Church Capitol Hill, Washington, D. C.; St. John's Church in West Hartford, Connecticut; St. Margaret's Church in Boiling Springs, South Carolina; and St. James Church in Wichita, Kansas. To the bishop who ordained me, the Rt. Rev. Clarence Coleridge, and to the Rt. Rev. Dorsey Henderson, my pastor and friend.

To my parents, to my two sons who have made my life so rich, and to my husband, my soulmate.